Two Plays of Weimar Germany

NORTHWESTERN WORLD CLASSICS

Northwestern World Classics brings readers
the world's greatest literature. The series features
essential new editions of well-known works,
lesser-known books that merit reconsideration,
and lost classics of fiction, drama, and poetry.
Insightful commentary and compelling new translations
help readers discover the joy of outstanding writing
from all regions of the world.

Ferdinand Bruckner

Two Plays of Weimar Germany

Youth Is a Sickness and *Criminals*

Translated from the German
by Laurence Senelick

Northwestern University Press ✦ *Evanston, Illinois*

Laurence Senelick

If you had asked an ordinary theatergoer in Weimar Berlin to name the best living German playwright, the answer would not have been "Bertolt Brecht" or "Georg Kaiser" or "Arnolt Bronnen." It would have been "Ferdinand Bruckner." Yet if asked, "Who is this Bruckner?," the Berliner would have been at a loss to give you any information.

In the late 1920s, the first two plays attributed to Bruckner, *Youth Is a Sickness* and *Criminals,* were hot tickets, but only gradually was the pseudonymous author identified. And then he turned out to be Theodor Tagger, a theater manager and playwright disdained for his bad business sense and uneven repertory choices.[1]

A Checkered Background

Theodor Tagger was born on 26 August 1891 in Sofia, Bulgaria, the son of a Viennese banker and businessman of Jewish antecedents. His mother, Claire Attias, a Frenchwoman born in Constantinople, was a translator devoted to art and literature. Young Tagger grew up in Vienna, and, after his parents' divorce, studied in a Jesuit college in Graz. Between 1909 and 1912, he alternated living with his mother in Paris and with his father in Berlin; he similarly divided his musical education between the Paris Conservatoire and the Berlin Hochschule für Musik, studying piano and composition under Franz Schreker, whose opera *Der ferne Klang* (1912) was considered the last word in musical experimentation. Music would remain one of Tagger's passions. He also began to write poetry in the styles of Hugo von Hofmannsthal, Rainer Maria Rilke, and Stefan George.

Tagger's musical and poetic activities displeased his father, who made him enter a school of international commerce in Berlin (Kafka and Wallace Stevens come to mind as fellow artists plugging away at commercial routines). To escape this unsympathetic environment and his father's demands, Tagger began to sit in on classes at the University of Vienna to study German literature and philology. He failed to graduate and moved back to Berlin but, to avoid going into his father's business, renounced any further paternal financial support.

Between 1910 and the outbreak of the Great War in 1914, Tagger took an active part in the cultural life of Berlin, writing articles for various German, Austrian, and Hungarian periodicals. In 1911 he published his own expressionistic journal and worked as a columnist and publisher's reader there and in Breslau. Lung problems kept him from being mobilized and sent him to a cure in Switzerland; in 1915 he dropped out of the Israelitische Kultusgemeinde (Jewish community) in Vienna, an emblematic divorce from his Jewish ancestry. This period of his life was marked, as it was for many of his contemporaries, by an attraction to an irrationality inspired by Richard Wagner, Arthur Schopenhauer, and Friedrich Nietzsche. At the same time, a core of patriotism motivated him to offer an apology for the fraught situation of a world at war. He attempted to establish a clear distinction between "the German spirit" and "the German Reich."

In 1917 Tagger published his first books, the novella *Die Vollendung eines Herzen* (Perfecting a heart) and the poetry collection *Der Herr in den Nebeln* (The gentleman in the clouds). With the theater critic Manfred George (né Cohn), he founded a bimonthly review, *Marsyas*, to which he managed to attract the foremost names in German and Austrian literature: Thomas Mann, Hofmannsthal, Hermann Hesse, Gottfried Benn, Alfred Döblin, Stefan Zwieg, Arthur Schnitzler, and Carl Sternheim, all of whom he befriended. The journal's eclecticism combined Tagger's fondness for irrationality and expressionism with a vague socialism and distaste for pan-German velleities. At the same time, a pietistic strain surfaced in his translations of Blaise Pascal and the Psalms of David for a large publishing firm.

The postwar period transformed Tagger from a rarefied writer aiming at a select circle of initiates, the author of self-consciously philosophic essays, into a champion of innovative, indeed revolutionary drama. Convinced that the theater was a medium peculiarly adapted to contribute to the development of "mass culture" at a time when parliamentary democracy was finding its feet in the German-speaking world, he returned to Vienna in 1919 to serve as a dramaturg at the Kammerspiele (chamber theater) of the Deutsches Volkstheater. In the German theater the function of dramaturg is far more influential than it is in the English-speaking world. He is the theater's literary manager, helping to shape the repertoire, creating or commissioning translations and adaptations, and writing the program notes. In addition, he is an equal member of the producing team, consulting with the director and *Intendant*, or producer, on major decisions about the theater's direction or a production's style.

In 1920 Tagger married Bettina Neuer and applied for Austrian citizenship. His earliest dramatic effort was a diptych of modern life, *Harry* and *Annette*. First produced at the Halle Municipal Theater, it reflected the profiteering and moneygrubbing rampant in the young republic. The next year Tagger, his wife, and their baby son moved back to Berlin, where he carried on his dramaturgical work for the Neues Theater am Zoo, and in 1922 he and Bettina founded the Renaissance Theater, in a cinema in the Hardenbergstrasse near the Bahnhof Zoo.

Between October 1922 and October 1927, Tagger produced forty-five plays there, nineteen of them staged by himself, and adapted a number of classics. Given that the German theater was at this time fermenting with radical experimentation, his choice of repertoire was idiosyncratic. Almost no prominent contemporary playwright appears in it: no card-carrying expressionist like Ernst Toller or Ernst Barlach or Oskar Kokoschka, no chronicler of the current scene like Fritz von Unruh or Franz Werfel, no political activist like Georg Kaiser or Bertolt Brecht, let alone such earlier masters as Frank Wedekind or Carl Sternheim. True, the theater opened with a classic, G. E. Lessing's *Miss Sara Sampson*; August Strindberg, Gabriele D'Annunzio, Anton Chekhov, and Leonid Andreev were undertaken, but, more surprisingly, so were such French boulevard dramatists as Louis Verneuil, Henri Lenormand, and Henri Bataille, perhaps in support of a Franco-German

one had read the *Neue Freie Presse,* one would have found that the play exhibited the "exhibitionistic audacity of the connoisseur," whereas a perusal of the *Reichspost* would have informed one that it was simply "psychic dung." Otto König defended the author in the *Arbeiter-Zeitung:* "The work in any case has striking poetic qualities. For a beginner's work there is a dazzlingly sure mastery of the stage, skillful construction, tight, psychologically well-developed dialogue, real people of flesh and blood."

The play was also staged, appropriately enough, at the Raimund Theater; its director, the critic Franz Theodor Csokor, and the young actor Walter Franck, ignorant of its authorship, urged Tagger to put it on in Berlin.[3] Tagger refused, saying it was too risky. The irony is that if Tagger had sponsored his pseudonymous work, it might have saved his management. Refurbishing the theater in Art Deco style in 1926 had entailed great expense, which a weak box office had not been able to meet. Debts had forced him to turn the Renaissance Theater over to Gustav Hartung and move to the Theater am Kurfürstendamm.

Hartung had an initial success with a comedy, *Coeur-Bube* (Knave of hearts), and began looking for something similar. Frederick Lonsdale's society drama *Aren't We All?* was under contract and already cast, but Hartung had misgivings about following in Tagger's path of least resistance. A Max Reinhardt pupil with a taste for expressionism, he decided that works of greater literary worth would bring in the public. According to Rudolph S. Joseph, the theater's dramaturg, a friend suggested that Hartung put on *Youth Is a Sickness.* An offbeat theater agency, Die Schmiede, had sent a copy of the play, which had already been accepted by Reinhardt, but with no production announced. (Reinhardt was one of the few who knew Bruckner's real identity.) Hartung read the typescript in its yellow binder and immediately saw his way to casting it, but when a reporter asked him who this Ferdinand Bruckner was, he had no idea. Die Schmiede directed him to the owner of the rights, Frau Tagger; she informed him that Bruckner was a young physician who lived with a patient in Rheims. Hartung made no further inquiries. However, during rehearsals he accidentally ran into Frau Tagger, who reproached him for ruining a young author's play because he had cast an actress already under contract whom she considered unsuited for the part. Hartung was annoyed; the Taggers had been incapable of running the Renaissance Theater, and now they were telling him how to do things.

The stage setting, an unprepossessing student common room, had to be reconciled with the Renaissance Theater's stylish auditorium. To save money, no designer was hired or furniture rented; the necessities were bought cheaply at a flea market. The centerpiece was an old-fashioned plush sofa, redyed in various shades of red; the woodwork was repainted in shades of brown, the walls in nuanced shades of green, meant to evoke an Impressionist painting. Over the sofa hung a large, inexpensive reproduction of Rembrandt's *Anatomy of Dr. Tulp*, purchased at a nearby framer's shop and stained with cold tea.

The Berlin opening took place on 26 April 1928. Hartung had put together a cast that, in age, personality, and way of life, mirrored the characters. Themselves a cross-section of Weimar youth, the actors made up a persuasively erotic ensemble. This included Elisabeth Lennartz (1902–2001), Hartung's wife and a friend of Marlene Dietrich, as Marie. The bisexual countess Desiree was played by Anni Mewes (1896–1980), an iconic flapper; her sculptural mask by Edwin Scharff was the most popular portrait sculpture of its time.[4] Erika Meingast (1901–72), the disapproving medical student Irene, was later the lover of the cabaret singer Marianne Oswald. Hans Adalbert von Scheltow (1887–1945), the cynical seducer Freder, was to play Hagen in Fritz Lang's film *Die Nibelungen*; an enthusiastic anti-Semite and eventual Nazi, he would die in a bombing raid. The Dutchman Gillis van Rappard (1899–1946), born in Java, played Petrell, alias Boysie; he was a charismatic and handsome, if somewhat effete, juvenile. The saturnine Gustav Diessi (1901–48), an erstwhile designer later to incarnate Jack the Ripper in F. W. Murnau's film *Die Büchse der Pandora*, and a friend of both Louise Brooks and Leni Riefenstahl, was cast as Alt, the philosophical kibitzer. As the Bavarian maid, Hilde Körber (1906–69) was not right for the part, according to Frau Tagger; her figure was lumpy and her teeth rather prominent, and offstage she wore a man's overcoat and a monocle, identifying tokens of a lesbian. Because of her eccentricity, she was rarely used in important roles, but she had a muffled, sensitive voice and expressive eyes. Körber was singled out for applause and by calls of her name as the discovery of the evening.[5] Overnight she became a much sought-after actress and, later, the second wife of Veit Harlan, notorious director of Nazi propaganda films, among them *Jew Süss*.

The Berlin critics showed off their learning by listing Bruckner's sources and forerunners—Strindberg, Wedekind, Andreev, Hans Henny Jahnn, and Bronnen—and they professed themselves unshocked by the now familiar psychological and sexual anomalies. Even the most negative, however, had to admire the play's terseness and racy dialogue, drawn from real life, not smacking of literature. "In the rather large tribe of the up-to-date sexual pathologists who have stormed the stage, Ferdinand Bruckner is definitely the most mature in talent and creative power." So pronounced Max Hochdorf in *Der Abend* (27 April 1928); and Harry Kahn, in the liberal *Die Weltbühne* (no. 18, 1928), delivered the following verdict: "This effect is chiefly the result of a spiritually tense, dramatically active dialogue, which, without lyric twaddle, goes right to the point and yet is not without poetic brilliance. All in all 'Youth Is a Sickness' is by far the most important theater play that this season . . . has brought forth."

The success was immediate for Hartung as manager and director, for the young actors, and for the mysterious Ferdinand Bruckner. But who was Bruckner? The disapproving review in the *Deutsche Zeitung* (28 April 1928) echoed Frau Tagger's explanation in referring to "a clandestine writer, of whom it is alleged that he holds his theatrical clearance sale after his medical consulting hours." Few believed this canard. The next season, no less an impresario than Reinhardt acquired Bruckner's second play, *Die Verbrecher* (*Criminals*), for his Deutsches Theater but refrained from directing it himself. Heinz Hilpert's excellent production was a success, which made the search for the author's identity even more frantic. High prices were offered for the information, detectives were employed, and one Berlin journalist pretended to be Bruckner in order to force him from his concealment. Margarete Anton, remembering Tagger's earlier poetry, thought him a likely candidate, but few were willing to attribute such good plays to such an inept director and manager.

Hartung, who had been pipped at the post by Reinhardt in acquiring the rights to *Criminals*, applied to Bruckner's publisher, S. Fischer, for the rights to Bruckner's third, yet unwritten play, but again the play was assigned to Reinhardt. When Hartung sued Fischer, Frau Tagger was named as Bruckner's agent. The lawyer for the Renaissance Theater, suspecting the author's identity, sent her a note: "Is it by Ferdinand Bruckner or Herr Tagger?" "It is by Bruckner, no, it is by my husband—it is therefore by Bruckner."

Now the secret was out. Tagger had used a pseudonym, partly because he knew that many in the profession had a low opinion of him, both for his mismanagement and for his feud with Brecht. These animosities might have prejudiced success. Moreover, a Herr Bruckner could bank his royalties unbeknownst to Tagger's creditors. A grotesque situation had arisen as a result: when he settled up with the Jakob-Michael-Konzern for debts he had contracted as former lessee of the Renaissance Theater, he had to hear from the general manager: "You had the theater for years without any success. No sooner has Herr Hartung taken it over, Herr Joseph uncovers *Youth Is a Sickness*. Why couldn't you have had this success?" Tagger was unable to say, "I am Ferdinand Bruckner.'" His earnings and his renown might both have been in jeopardy. Even with his anonymity blown, he never attended rehearsals or opening nights of his plays until *Timon* was produced at the Vienna Burgtheater in 1932. He did not make an appearance onstage *in propria persona* until the Viennese premiere of *Elisabeth von England* (Elizabeth of England), when he was greeted with tempestuous applause.

Diagnosing the Disease of Being Young

When Bruckner published a collection of his plays, in 1945, he gave it the generic title *Jugend zweier Kriege* (The youth of two wars), a diagnosis of the pathology of two generations engendered and deformed by war. In *Youth Is a Sickness*, the "malady of youth" directly results from World War I and what fed it. Pubescent during the 1914–18 war, Bruckner's characters can barely make sense of it, and in the ensuing period they have to face a great void—moral, intellectual, spiritual, social, economic, political—created by the traumata, defeat, and disappointed hopes of the Spartacist Revolt and the early Weimar Republic. Driven into a corner by the prospect of "no future," as foretold by the abandonment of age-old certainties, they reject the traditional family structure and grope for some kind of meaningful relationship among themselves. Such relationships—overwrought emotionally, highly sexualized, physically brutal—are carried on at such a fever pitch that they can end only in disaster. Death is the ultimate stimulant for lives that lack plan, aim, sense, and value. In this play, Bruckner's high-pitched expressionism reaches such a climax as to teeter toward existentialism.

Sex, so frankly treated, is no joyous release but ravages the characters in all their games, ambivalent teasing, and refined inhibitions. The function of the dialogue is to have them analyze each another ruthlessly and voluptuously, stripping away in an orgy of schadenfreude the last shabby rags of dignity and illusion. The emotions shuttle between exultant passion and frigid repulsion, their origins unrecognizable in the heart or in the head. Bruckner's diagnostic, laconic style had been influenced by Georg Büchner, whose *Danton's Death* (1835) had had its first performances in the decade before the war. In Bruckner, however, the tempestuous rhetoric contrasted with cool rationality is transferred from the public sphere to the intimacy of private lives.

Bruckner chose to set the play not in Berlin but in Vienna, a milieu he was familiar with from his student days, but which had not undergone the same hard times that Germany had. This dislocation places more emphasis on the psychologies of the characters themselves; whatever the loss of values in society, their egocentrism and narcissism are what motivate the action. Bruckner keeps the theme of sickness in sight by making his female characters medical students. They gabble nihilist philosophies, dabble in the drug *du jour*, stray from bed to bed, and end up with death wishes and suicide pacts. At no point do they talk of alleviating pain or serving humanity.

Throughout his dramatic work, Bruckner's women provide the balance: he enjoys letting them live, love, suffer, go off the rails, destroy and be destroyed, even rant and rave, but never against their nature, because this is the be-all and end-all for them. This emotional release must never be questioned or lost, yet in Bruckner it clashes with an irreconcilable maternal drive. Marie, the "ambitious farm girl from Passau," has supported both the dilettante Petrell and the pansexual Desiree; Irene is eager to take Petrell over from Marie, though she denies it. Desiree's fondest memory is of sleeping with her little sister. Only the maid turned streetwalker, Lucie, seems incapable of caring for someone else; she is putty in the hands of a stronger will, happy to submit.

In Bruckner's plays, the women's world is compulsively roiled by men, the fanatics, deceivers, idle and unconscionable egocentrics, or else idealists and misogynists, who shamelessly exploit and plunder them. The men are more schematic in their depiction—Freder the ultra-aggressive, Petrell the ultra-passive and Alt, rendered so impotent by past experience that he clings to the sidelines; they exist only insofar as the women respond to them.

None of Bruckner's women can reproach herself for letting slip an opportunity to live. They may ultimately toss life away, but never before they have lived it. They may even set an example. "It's never the things that matter that lay us low," says Alt, a line that, for Bruckner's women, holds the key to their tragedy. When they are laid low, it is always for something unimportant, inconsequential. In the *danse macabre* of diseased youth, Marie is carefully reserved for the gruesome final figure: she will let Freder bite through her throat. She has done all she can for her little menagerie, and all she asks is thanks. Loyalty is the chord of her life. What withers in others, blooms in her. That her beloved Petrell is a zero changes nothing in her love, even as it makes her miserable.

A Criminal in Every Room

Although it developed certain themes already present in *Harry*, *Annette*, and *Youth Is a Sickness*, the immediate impetus for *Criminals* seems to have been Bruckner's attendance at a performance of Toller's *Hoppla wir leben!* (Hurray, we're alive!). Erwin Piscator's staging at the Theater am Nollendorfplatz was based on the principle of simultaneous action, and its functional setting, designed by

Traugott Müller, was a massive scaffolding demarcated into eight acting areas and a revolving stage.[6] *Criminals*, published by S. Fischer in late September 1927, presented in two of its acts the cross-section of an apartment building, with seven rooms on three levels. The lights would come up on those segments of the set where the action was taking place. The setting for the central act allowed for four separate trials to take place and comment ironically on each other. Bruckner, with his Viennese background, may have been familiar with Johann Nestroy's comedy *Zu ebener Erde und im ersten Stock* (Ground floor and first floor, 1835), which anticipated this device, albeit in a simpler form.

Criminals was fortunate in its first director, for Heinz Hilpert (1890–1967), who had served for three years as an assistant to Reinhardt at the Deutsches Theater, had imbibed his boss's penchant for theatricality. He had also learned from Reinhardt's master, Otto Brahm, whose Freie Bühne (Free Stage) had been dedicated to principles of realism and social purpose. Hilpert was similarly devoted to objective verisimilitude and a spirit of ensemble. The cast for *Criminals* was outstanding. Lucie Höflich (1882–1956), who played the cunning cook Ernestine Puschek, had been brought by Reinhardt from Vienna to incarnate Margarethe in *Faust*; she also excelled in the plays of Gerhart Hauptmann and Henrik Ibsen. Opposite her as the lady-killer Gustav Tunichtgut was Hans Albers (1891–1960), who had worked with Piscator; a virile leading man with good comic technique, he would become Germany's favorite film actor. The bisexual Gustaf Gründgens (1899–1963) was perfectly cast as the cynical Ottfried; a mime, dancer, and cabaret artiste as well as a versatile actor, he tended to be showy. Originally associated with leftist circles, he later came to an accommodation with the Nazis and was pilloried for it in the novel *Mephisto* by his former lover Klaus Mann. The rest of the company was equally strong, with experienced character actors in even the smallest roles. The production, which opened on 23 October 1928, with scenery by Rochus Gliese and Friedrich Ulmer, was a palpable hit and turned out to be the greatest success of the Deutsches Theater in the 1920s.

Criminals received far more attention and more polarized opinion than *Youth Is a Sickness*, in part because many journalists were piqued by the continuing mystery of Bruckner's identity. The nay-sayers among the critics included the influential Herbert Ihering (*Berliner Börsen-Courier*, 24 October 1928), who described it as *Youth Is a Sickness–cum–*Piscator, another banal rehash of Wede-kind and Bronnen. Dr. Richard Biedrzynski (pseudonym of Alfred Mühr, *Deutsche Zeitung*, evening edition, 24 October 1928) de-nounced it as "Untimely, anti-social, sophisticated, phony and men-dacious [. . .] It is naturalism vintage 1928 with a political message." Paul Fechter (*Deutsche Allgemeine Zeitung*, evening edition, 24 Oc-tober 1928) dismissed it as "even less important than *Youth Is a Sick-ness.*" As for the ingenious staging, Monty Jacobs in the *Vossische Zeitung* (25 October 1928) downgraded it as an unacknowledged plagiarism of Johann Nestroy and the Kreisler stage of Carl Mein-hard and Rudolf Bernauer.[7] And its message was Tolstoy for dum-mies: "Men should not judge men!"

These negative appraisals constituted a minority report. Most of the press recognized and praised the play's topicality, didacticism, and excitement.[8] Sure, Bruckner had taken advantage of the cinema, the Kreisler stage, even Kaiser's *Side by Side*, admitted the left-wing *Die Weltbühne* (Harry Kahn, no. 44, 1928), but the result was not eclectic but an idiosyncratic conveyance of the message: "As much as anyone, Bruckner is a modern and original stage talent of high rank; and as much as anywhere, here is the onset of that 'epic drama' which the sloganeers and trend-setters foretell on every inappro-priate occasion." The enigmatic Bruckner was praised as a man with his ear to the ground, capable of transcribing vividly and accurately the zeitgeist into a "stenogram of reality" (Fritz Engel, *Berliner Tageblatt*, 24 October 1928; Ernst Hellborn, *Frankfurter Zeitung*, evening edition, 25 October 1928). Tagger's former collaborator Manfred George saw beyond the immediacy of the contemporary reportage to describe the play as a tragedy of fate unfolding in an apartment house, the destinies of the tenants inextricably bound together (*Tempo*, 24 October 1928). The ensemble performance was lauded as being of the highest order, with the leads in top form but even the smallest walk-on making an impression (*Berliner Mon-tagsblatt*, 29 October 1928; Norbert Falk, *BZ am Mittag*, 24 October 1928).

There were appeals to the censor. A production planned for the Munich Kammerspiele in 1929, with the remarkable actress Therese Giehse as Ernestine, was permitted to proceed only as a closed dress rehearsal and then set aside. The first Austrian production opened on 18 April 1929 at the Theater in der Josefstadt, with Lucie Höflich and Gustaf Gründgens repeating their roles as Ernestine and Ottfried. In this Catholic city, the play was very coolly received. *Welt am Montag* (20 April 1929) said that "Bruckner's dream quagmire [was] only to be passed over rapidly like a nightmare," while *Kleines Volkblatt* (20 April 1929) called it a "repulsive sensation play."

The critic Rudolf Holzer had pointed out that Bruckner's interest in the methods of staging the play might be a deficit, more cerebral than emotional; but he argued that the same charge could be lodged against Shakespeare. The devices were intended to drive home the ideas that activated the play. One of Bruckner's early cheerleaders, the Austrian critic Csokor, was later (1955) to insist that the dramatist was driven by an inner mission: "In an era of push and management he remained the rare example of a writer who saw his creations not as wares but as warnings and means, meant to pose new questions in an imperfect world." The hostile charge that Bruckner dealt in "gimmicks"—simultaneous action, multilevel stage sets, ironic musical accompaniment—might also be aimed at the innovations of Brecht's "epic theater." In both cases, the intent was to encompass the vast complexities of an era's political and cultural life.

Some theater historians have cited *Criminals* as, if not the first, then the prime example of the *Zeitstück*, or topical play, which dominated German stages in the 1920s and 1930s.[9] In a context marked by galloping capitalism and stifled democracy, a bloodily repressed Communist revolution, and periodic governmental and economic crises, the events of the day had to be addressed. The *Zeitstück* confronted issues raised by defeatism and anarchy; the cynicism, opportunism, or nihilistic pessimism of the younger generation; the gap between the law, on the one hand, and social progress, sexual liberation, and class conflict, on the other. At the same time, the artistic scene was marked by an irrepressible effervescence, in the realms of both playwriting and stagecraft. The play of the present day had to be cast in a form attractive and pertinent to an informed audience avid for the latest thing. Bruckner, like his friend and colleague Odön von Horváth, felt called upon to question the existing social order and explore the conflict between morality and sexual compulsion. However, in his case, the social-critical element goes hand in hand with his journalistic way of thinking and his familiarity with psychoanalytic theory. Modernist, progressive, yet deeply pessimistic, Bruckner's early plays have a strongly polemical character.

Exceptionally talented at dramatic construction and dialogue, in *Criminals* Bruckner focuses on the issue of justice and the contradiction between the life principle and the law. It was a not uncommon dramatic theme at the time: Alexandre Bisson's *Madame X*, John Galsworthy's *The Silver Box*, and a host of American courtroom dramas (*On Trial* by Elmer Rice, 1914; *The Trial of Mary Dugan* by Bayard Veiller, 1927) made it a familiar device. Bruckner's originality lay in his panoramic view of society, each of the four specific cases shedding light on another. Each is a miscarriage of justice. An innocent if unsavory man is convicted of a murder on circumstantial evidence, while the real murderer goes free. A thief from a respectable family is acquitted because of his good attitude. A failed suicide is convicted of infanticide. A homosexual youth, compelled to give evidence in favor of a blackmailer, is himself arrested because of the infamous section 175 of the penal code, which condemned sexual relations between men. Since the beginning of the twentieth century, there had been militant protest to revoke that clause, but to no effect; it stayed in force under the Weimar Republic, the Nazis, and the Bundesrepublik. Meanwhile, lechers, blackmailers, abortionists, and other social offenders carried on with impunity.

Despite the somewhat tendentious nature of the scenes in the judges' chambers, *Criminals* is neither a *pièce à these* in the style of Eugène Brieux nor a debate in the style of Bernard Shaw. Nor it is a Brechtian *Lehrstück*, with its ethical questions emblazoned in capital letters. The discussions agitating the adolescent Weimar Republic are embodied in characters from everyday life, identifiable human beings at grips with a system—in this case, the legal system—that runs roughshod over anyone without the force of character or cynicism to face it down or exploit it. Even when some of the social issues—such as the criminality of sex between men, private adoption, or abortion—are no longer so problematic, the dramatic power of the situations and characters and the formal inventiveness of the dramatic structure make *Criminals* one of the most powerful plays of the first half of the twentieth century.

The chief miscarriage of justice has less to do with the legal code than with the elemental passions of a working-class woman. Once again, Bruckner's women, often creatures of impulse and passion, stubborn and blind and monomaniacal to the point of perjury, are motivated—paradoxical as it may sound—by the maternal instinct. The gamut of maternity runs in this play from Frau von Wieg, ineffectual and ignorant, to Frau Berlessen, sacrificing her dignity to her erotic interest in her sons' friend; from Olga Nagerle, so desperate to keep her baby that she contemplates a double suicide, to Mimi Zerl, who reluctantly pays for an abortion. Ernestine Puschek's faked pregnancy precipitates much of the fatal outcome; her desire to pass off another's child as her own to hang on to her lover, and her abrupt renunciation of that aim, have dire consequences.

In a lecture titled "On the Essence of the Tragic," Bruckner defines the tragic as "the contrast in every human being between the individual he is and the member of a community that he is at the same time, whether this community is a people or a society or a communion in God or only a relationship between man and wife: there is in every human breast a Self that is and wants to be an individual and will be nothing else, facing a Self, its companion, that is a portion of something else and must be whether it will or no." Tunichtgut speaks for almost all Bruckner's male characters when to the judge's remark "You had at that time five lovers simultaneously" he casually replies, "Any self-respecting man would. I was always a perfect gentleman." For all his vaunted virility, he has to be defined by the women in his life, and, as with the Greeks, woman stands for the dark Dionysian world. Even as the smug, snappy ladies' man stumbles unsuspecting to his doom, Ernestine has no need to shove, merely nudge.

In its own way, *Criminals* is no more realistic than *Youth Is a Sickness*. Otherwise Bruckner would have left his Tunichtgut, brought to the gallows by false witness, a loophole to slip through, for the waiter, though obtuse about his own situation, is no fool. Instead, Bruckner lets him die. In the process, this slick, streetwise lothario takes on the allure of a tragic hero. What makes the courtroom scenes in *Criminals* so fascinating is not the crucifixion of Tunichtgut through a judicial error that can brand anyone a criminal, because, as the younger judge has pointed out, the law presupposes criminality in a human being. Bruckner effectively manages to denounce that essential failing in the law. However, the fascination of those scenes lies in the fall of a man whose ingenuous lust for life, whose self-defense mechanisms, are so fatally damaged that he cannot see the malevolent potential in his fellow humans, be they judge, defense attorney, or fiancée.

Ernestine Puschek is too big for the frame of a standard courtroom drama; she takes on the mantle of Justice itself, relying on the ancient legal argument of an eye for an eye. Were she only a jealous cook who murders a rival and lays the blame on her lover out of revenge, the legal proceedings would have no special interest. What elevates *Criminals* to a tragic level is the way that the ostensible figure of strength and control, Tunichtgut, blindly falls into the trap laid for him.

Despite the absence of women in the homosexual subplot, allegedly feminine sentiments motivate the youths. Ottfried is one of the earliest theatrical avatars of a type already familiar in fiction: the feline manipulator. Here, at any rate, his callousness derives from his unreciprocated love for Frank. Frank is another cliché: bookish, weak-willed, a bundle of nerves, sexually obsessed, a ready-made victim. Just as Freder leads Lucie into prostitution, so Ottfried urges Frank to perjure himself; but whereas Lucie, with her earthy feminine stability, thrives on the streets, Frank, a womanish man, falls to pieces. For all the attack on section 175, Bruckner is careful not to make its victims heroic or militant.

Although *Criminals* found a place on foreign stages sooner than did *Youth Is a Sickness*, the latter play's continued success and regular revival indicate that its symptoms are not limited to the period between the wars; the disaffection of youth and its self-destructive behavior are recurrent and international phenomena. The émigré Georgian actor/director Georges Pitoëff mounted the play with his company at the Théâtre des Arts in Paris; it achieved two hundred performances over several months in 1929. In 1931 an improvised troupe of German actors living in Paris gave *Youth Is a Sickness* for the first time in French (as *Mal de la Jeunesse*) at the Studio des Champs-Élysées. The play was revived the same year at the Théâtre de l'Œuvre by the Belgian troupe of Raymond Rouleau, with Tania Balachova and Madeleine Ozeray among others, then revived in 1932 by the same team, again to achieve over two hundred performances. The international renown of Ferdinand Bruckner was then at its apogee. Thanks to these two plays, Bruckner played an important part in the intervention of the stage in raging debates on such questions as sexual liberation, the role of justice, and the nature of the penal law.

The Price of Fame

In the wake of these two hits, Bruckner had a setback with *Die Kreatur* (The creature, 1929). Despite first-rate productions staged by leading directors—Reinhardt at the Berlin Komödie Theater, and Otto Falckenburg at the Munich Kammerspiele—and strong casts, this morbid psychosexual drama of a failed marriage put off critics and audiences alike. At the Munich premiere a man in the first row stood up, leaned over the stage, and vomited at the feet of the leading actor.[10]

Turning his back on the *Zeitstück*, Bruckner chose to use the past as a mirror of the present. *Elisabeth von England* became the blockbuster of the 1930–31 season in a staging by Gustav Hartung, with Agnes Straub as the queen, Werner Krauss as Philip of Spain, Adolf Wohlbrück (soon to be the refugee Anton Walbrook) as Essex, and Gustaf Gründgens as Bacon. Mounted on a split stage, it contrasted the policy decisions of England and Spain simultaneously, with obvious reference to the prevailing political situation in Europe. The Inquisition was a clear counterpart to the Gestapo. Hailed as a masterpiece, the play bestowed on Bruckner a fame surpassing that of Brecht and Carl Zuckmayer. He was now the most celebrated, most popular playwright in the Weimar Republic. With *Elisabeth von En-*

gland translated into seventeen languages, his name spread beyond the German-speaking world. In Ashley Dukes's adaptation *Gloriana*, it played for five months at the Cambridge Theatre. Bruckner had managed to develop a style that allowed him to come to grips with the turmoil of his era and take part in the sociopolitical maturity of his country.

Bruckner was alert to the lowering political atmosphere. His second son, Andreas, was born in 1932, and in February of the following year, in the aftermath of the Reichstag fire, Bruckner took his family to Vienna for the Austrian premiere of *Die Marquise von O.*, his adaptation of Heinrich von Kleist's story. They did not return to Germany but emigrated through Zurich and Prague to Paris. Hitler's rise to power motivated Bruckner to evolve in his work from a critique of German society to an "engaged humanism." He turned from a commentator with reformist tendencies to a political militant, whose ideas resembled those of the Popular Front. This development was heralded by an unabashedly antifascist play *Die Rassen* (The races, 1933), an acute analysis of life in Nazi Germany.[11] Its accuracy was all the more surprising, since he had to rely on reports from friends and associates still in the homeland. *Die Rassen* was produced at the Zurich Schauspielhaus on 30 November 1933. The play was such an indictment of the National Socialist platform that a proposed English production was prohibited by the Lord Chamberlain, which prompted a protest from the Pen Club. Bruckner's antifascism was all-out: he severed all relations with Germany, withdrawing the rights for his plays to be performed on German stages. Friends who tried to ignore the "bad side" of Hitler's regime while keeping their minds and spirits intact provoked nothing but scorn.

Like so many antifascist emigrants, Bruckner had to keep one step ahead of Hitler's *Wehrmacht*. He traveled to London in 1935 to meet with Alexander Korda about a film based on *Elisabeth von England*. The deal fell through, and instead Korda adapted A. E. Mason's novel *Fire Over England* (1936) for his patriotic Armada movie (though elements of Bruckner's drama can still be discerned in it). Otto Preminger invited Bruckner to California, so in March 1936 Bruckner sailed for New York and made his way to Hollywood, where his train was met by Ernst Lubitsch and Peter Lorre (who would later play his Napoleon on Broadway). Despite this promising beginning, none of Bruckner's screenplays was found workable, so he returned to New York in 1937.

The next year Dukes's *Gloriana* was staged at the Little Theatre in New York, with limited success. The reason is not far to seek. It had been preempted by Maxwell Anderson's *Elizabeth the Queen*, produced by the Theatre Guild in 1930 as a vehicle for Alfred Lunt and Lynn Fontanne, which enjoyed a run of one hundred forty-seven performances. Both Bruckner and Anderson had been inspired by Lytton Strachey's *Elizabeth and Essex: A Tragic History* (1928), but their approaches could not have been more different. Anderson's play, written in the blankest of blank verse, is a fancy-dress love story set against a backdrop of historical events. Bruckner's, inspired by Piscator, is a world-historical epic, contrasting two methods of governance. In America, any chance that Bruckner's play might get an objective hearing would also be jinxed by *Fire Over England* and the Hollywood film of 1939 *The Private Lives of Elizabeth and Essex,* very loosely based on Strachey, with Bette Davis and Errol Flynn in the title roles.

Throughout his time in New York, Bruckner remained close to the German-language emigrant community and took a leading role in its political efforts. He lectured at Brooklyn and Queens Colleges; in early October 1938 he was named copresident of the German American Writers Association, and in May 1939 he attended the extraordinary PEN Congress (two years later he was a founding member of European PEN in America). The left-leaning New School for Social Research sponsored the Dramatic Workshop, headed by Piscator; in 1940 Bruckner was hired as its professor of dramaturgy.

This official position gave impetus to productions of his work; the Washington Square Players staged *Maladies of Youth* in New York in 1941. On 20 December of that year *Criminals* was performed in Piscator's Studio Theatre, directed by Sanford Meisner, recently of the Group Theatre, and with the Hungarian actress Lili Darvas, another Reinhardt alumna, making her American debut. The timing was terrible, since this was two weeks after the bombing of Pearl

Harbor and the entrance of the United States into World War II. Beyond that, the translation, credited to Edwin Denby and Rita Matthias, was a drastically abridged version, in which the homosexual plot was transformed into an anti-Nazi intrigue. The cast was cut in half, the seven stage spaces were reduced to four, and the dialogue was toned down and packed with euphemisms and current slang. The reference to Stendhal was replaced by a reference to Freud. For the most part, the reviewers were respectful. Rosamund Gilder of *Theater Arts* magazine found it an interesting play about pre-Nazi Germany, though she was bemused by the actors' addressing of the audience (a Piscator touch not in the original). *Billboard* (3 January 1942) dismissed it as "an ineffective hodgepodge." The American stage was still not ready for devices that were commonplace on the German stage of the 1920s. *Criminals* closed after fifteen performances. (Bruckner's replacement of the homosexual plot with an anti-Nazi intrigue was retained in the first German anthology of his plays, published by Aufbau-Verlag in 1949. This, along with the existence of a typescript of the Dramatic Workshop version, has led uninformed reviewers to wonder at Bruckner's prescience in predicting Nazi tactics and dominance as early as 1928.)

A reading of *Die Rassen*, adapted by Berthold Viertel, was offered at the Tribune for Free German Literature and Art in America. In March 1942 Bruckner translated and adapted *Nathan der Weise* for the Studio Theatre, the first Lessing play to be performed in English on an American stage. During his time in the United States, Bruckner wrote eleven plays, three film scenarios, and an outline for another play. He translated four of his plays into English and *Death of a Salesman* into German. In addition, he wrote for several papers and magazines: *Austro-American Tribune*; *Aufbau* (founded and edited by his old friend Manfred George); *Freies Deutschland*; and *The German-American*, organ of the German American Writers Association. In late 1944 he was a founding member of the publishing house Aurora-Verlag, with Wieland Herzfelde, Bertolt Brecht, Berthold Viertel, and other representatives of the German literary community.

At the defeat of Germany, Bruckner composed *Die Befreiten* (The liberated, 1945), which confronts the American "liberators" with Germans traumatized by Nazism and presciently suggests how difficult the return to democracy will be. Now an American citizen, in 1946 he joined Players from Abroad, a troupe that included the former German matinee idol Hans Jaray, Albert and Elsie Bassermann, and Paul Henreid. From 1948 on, however, he was looking homeward and communicating with European circles, particularly the French Institute in Vienna.

Bruckner's importance had not been forgotten at home. The critic Rudolf Holzer in 1948 praised him as "probably the dramatist of the epoch, a real, absolute dramatist, a builder of plays, who knows how to use all means to achieve theatrical effects." Bruckner traveled to what was then West Berlin in March 1951 to assist Boleslav Barlog at the Schiller and Schlosspark Theaters as dramaturg; he moved to have his pseudonym recognized as his legal name. Since theaters were important agents in reestablishing prewar cultural values in Germany and Austria, his appointment signaled his status as a semiofficial representative of the anti-Nazi policies of the Federal Republic. He therefore embodied a more moderate liberal counterpart to Brecht, whose Berliner Ensemble had settled into the Theater am Schifferbauerdamm in East Berlin as the showplace for Communist playwriting. Bruckner returned to the topical play with *Früchte des Nichts* (The fruits of the void, 1951), a kind of existentialist road movie describing the wanderings of a group of young people the day after the war ended. They are divided between a radical nihilism and the absolute necessity to reconstruct a world. Bruckner had identified another lost generation and given them voice. One of his last plays, the blank-verse *Der Kampf mit dem Engel* (Wrestling with the angel, 1956), features an extraordinary woman who has cynically mastered the machinery of the stock exchange but is confronted by one of her sons-in-law with the spiritual superiority of a life devoted to others.

The first volume of a collected edition of his complete plays came out in 1956, and the following year Bruckner was presented with the Prize of the City of Vienna. He cofounded a dramatic workshop in Salzburg shortly before dying in Berlin of lung disease on 5 December 1958.

Afterlife

Bruckner is a prime example of what we now call a "public intellectual," a man whose life was devoted to reflecting on the fate of Germany, humane values, and the past, present, and future of a troubled century. Like many of his contemporaries, he was excited by the possibilities of the stage for addressing issues of war and peace, social and political problems, and the fate of contemporary youth with its lack of ideals and eternal nostalgia.[12] The relevance of Bruckner's dramas has been confirmed by the numerous revivals he enjoyed after the war. The first revival of *Krankheit der Jugend* was in its Italian premiere at the Teatro Excelsior, Milan, in 1947, and the next in Vienna at the Studio der Hochschulen (January 1949). The first London production, under the title *The Sickness of Youth*, had played at the Gate Theatre in 1934; the same theater revived it as *Pains of Youth* in 1987, in a translation by Daphne Moore, directed by Patti Love.

With its single setting and small youthful cast, the play has been a fixture in German repertories, but has almost always been updated. In 1968, a particularly fraught time for Germany, it was staged by Action-Theater, forerunner of the legendary Antiteater, in a production by Jean-Marie Straub; the cast included Rainer Werner Fassbinder. The version directed by Tilmen Köhler at the Deutsches National Theater Weimar was invited to Berlin's Theatertreffen in 2007. The same year, a contemporary adaptation was filmed by Michael Haneke, and in 2009 a ninety-one-minute, partly improvised, wholly modernized teleplay, under the direction of Dieter Berner, came out of Potsdam; the screenplay was attributed to Hilde Berger. Recently the play has attracted attention in the English-speaking world, with Martin Crimp's adaptation performed by the National Theatre, London, directed by Katie Mitchell (2009), and an Off-Off-Broadway production directed by Katie Lupica (2014). A production at the Paris Cartoucherie, staged by Philippe Baronnet (2016), was, as one critic noted, "a play of startling timeliness."

Since *Criminals* requires a more elaborate and expensive production, there have been fewer revivals. The first postwar production had to wait until February 1958, at the Schiller-Theater in West Berlin, directed by Hans Lietzau, a specialist in Eugène Ionesco and Jean Genet. In late 1981, East Berlin took cognizance of it at the Volksbühne, under the direction of Werner Tietze. Intended as an anniversary celebration, *The Criminals* was staged by Michael Kimmel at New York's Performance Space in 2001. The translation was attributed to Ann Crawford Flexner, most famous for her early twentieth-century dramatization of *Mrs. Wiggs of the Cabbage Patch*; she had indeed copyrighted a translation called *Law Breakers* in 1930, but it remained unpublished. From remarks by the reviewers, especially concerning "the rise of Nazism," it would appear that this production actually used the 1941 Studio Theatre version, with all its omissions, distortions, and alterations. Far more authentic was a stunning French staging by Richard Brunel, director of the Comédie de Valence, at the spacious Théâtre de la Colline in 2011. Employing a revolving stage with dividing panels and a cast of sixteen, his production was so revelatory that critics were led to refer to Bruckner as a forerunner of Georges Perec and his "la vie mode d'emploi." *Les Criminels* not only received a prize in 2013 for the best provincial production but also inspired the publication of new French translations of Bruckner's plays.

Notes

1. There is very little writing on Bruckner available in English. In German there are nearly a dozen dissertations, but no definitive life and works. Alfred Kantorowicz's biography (Berlin, 1947) appeared while the playwright was still alive; *Die Dramatiker Ferdinand Bruckner* by Christiane Lehfeldt (Göppingen, 1971) is now outdated. There is a published critical monograph of his early writing by Ingrid Rurl, *Aktualität und Tradition: Studien zu Ferdinand Bruckners Werk bis 1930* (Hamburg, 1995), and a collection of essays in German edited by Hans-Gert Roloff (Berlin, 2008). Fritz Schwiefert's article "Ferdinand Bruckner," *Maske und Kothurn* 4:4 (December 1958), 358–70, is also useful.

2. Klaus Völker, *Brecht a Biography*, trans. John Nowell (New York: Continuum, 1978), 107. The negative reviews included notices by Herbert

Ihering, *Berliner Börsen-Courier* (11 March 1925); Alfred Kerr, *Berliner Tageblatt*; and Monty Jacobs, *Vossische Zeitung*.

3. Franck had created Garga in Brecht's *Im Dickicht der Städte* (*In the Jungle of Cities*) and Gaul in Bronnen's *Anarchie in Sicilien*.

4. The Nazis exhibited it in their Degenerate Art Exhibition; lost during the bombing of Berlin, it was eventually found and badly reconstructed.

5. The calls were made by Bruno Adriani, an upper administrator of the ministry of culture, who let his enthusiasm override his professional objectivity; see Rudolph S. Joseph, *Aus grosser Theaterzeit: Erinnerungen an das Theater der zwanziger Jahre* (Alano Verlag, 1994). Also see Julius Bab in the morning edition of the *Berliner Volks-Zeitung* (28 April 1928).

6. Hugh Rorrison, "Piscator's *Hoppla wir leben!*," *Theatre Quarterly* 37 (1980).

7. The Kreisler-Bühne was Sven Gade's 1922 construction for *Die wunderlichen Geschichten der Kapellmeisters Kreisler*, which allowed for forty-two set changes in six separate acting areas, but without simultaneous action.

8. See, for example, Kurt Pinthus in *8-Uhr-Abendblatt* (24 October 1928).

9. Some critics translate *Zeitstück* as "documentary drama," but this is off the mark. A documentary drama, as defined by Erwin Piscator and the Soviet playwright Sergei Tretyakov, is a play based on specific current events, and its action is drawn from the journalism and documentation recording those events.

10. Ursula Cerlas, *Ewald Balser* (*1898–1978*) (Vienna: Böhlau, 2004), 80–82.

11. *Die Rassen* was, for obvious reasons, the first of Bruckner's plays to be translated into English and performed. As late as 2001 a powerful adaptation by Barry Edelstein was produced at CSC Repertory Theatre in New York.

12. Francis Cros, *Tagger/Bruckner, ambiguïtés modernistes et humanisme militant* (Nancy, 1984).

Youth Is a Sickness

✦ *A Play in Three Acts* ✦

CHARACTERS

MARIE
DESIREE
IRENE
FREDER
PETRELL
ALT
LUCY

The girls are all very young, the men somewhat older.

ACT I

[*As in the other two acts,* MARIE's *room in a boardinghouse.*]

SCENE 1

MARIE [*at the door to the hallway*]: You're going to make me late, Lucy.

LUCY [*offstage*]: Coming.

MARIE: Bring hot water.

[LUCY *enters with a bucket.*]

MARIE: You may go.

LUCY: You scrubbing floors?

MARIE [*scrubs the floor; laughing*]: Friday is my bachelorette party.

LUCY: A bachelorette party without a wedding.

MARIE [*laughs*]: Graduation is a kind of wedding.

[*Bell rings.*]

LUCY: Number 4 is calling for his breakfast.

[LUCY exits.]

MARIE [*works; after a while*]: Daisy. You still in bed?

DESIREE [*from her room*]: I'm washing.

MARIE [*again at the door to the hallway*]: Clean water for the windows. And a washrag.

LUCY [*from the hallway*]: Right away.

SCENE 2

[DESIREE *comes out of the adjoining room.*]

MARIE: Up so early?

DESIREE: Help me review. Here're the crib notes.

MARIE: What time do you go on?

DESIREE: 10:00.

MARIE [*carries on scrubbing*]: Read.

DESIREE: Lungs. [*She yawns, then stretches.*] Why get up so early?

MARIE: You have stage fright?

DESIREE: At the moment I don't feel a thing. Fine. [*Reads from notes.*] Advanced cavernous tuberculosis. In principle, cavernous tuberculosis does not differ from ordinary progressive tuberculosis, the formation of caverns being only a secondary effect of caseation. [*Sets down notes; laughs; puts her legs on the table.*] That kid Irene wants to bet me she'll be a doctor first, even though she's two semesters behind me.

MARIE [*still busy*]: Where do caverns form?

DESIREE [*reading again from notes*]: In the areas of the primary infection, the upper bronchials, and specifically in the subapical zones. [*Sets down notes.*] A nasty sort.

MARIE: She's ambitious, but pretty.

DESIREE: A red-haired fish. She'll go far.

MARIE: The smaller caverns . . .

DESIREE [*reading again from notes*]: The smaller caverns occur in relatively minor infections. [*Sets down notes.*] Freder's doing the maid.

MARIE [*aghast*]: Lucy?

DESIREE: I caught him slipping out of her room.

MARIE: The swine.

[DESIREE *laughs.*]

MARIE: That's why the girl's been depressed the last few days.

DESIREE [*laughs*]: And she limps.

MARIE: Lucy limps?

DESIREE: Whenever a woman gives in to a man who's her superior, she walks in a different way.

MARIE: You're kidding.

DESIREE: Out of fear. Pressure.

MARIE [*cautiously*]: What about you?

DESIREE: Oh, me. I've been over him a long time now.

MARIE: But you used to be mad about one another.

DESIREE [*laughs*]: Once upon a time . . . He was the first to prove to me that a man can be good for something. Down to the fingertips. Have to do him justice: he's not only strong, he's a virtuoso. [*Sighs.*] But you can get fed up even with a virtuoso.

MARIE [*simply*]: You have to be in love, or else you always get fed up.

DESIREE: Love? You call that love, with your bland Boysie?

MARIE [*laughs*]: Not as bland as all that!

DESIREE [*astonished*]: No? I can't imagine he has any idea of what a woman needs.

MARIE [*smiles*]: What does a woman need?

DESIREE [*approaches her*]: Only women know what women need. [*Affectionately*] Marion! I call you Marion, my sister's name. Those were the holiest moments in my life: when the governess said good-night, put out the light and left. I would quickly creep into Marion's bed, we would lie there, pressed together, kissing, feeling the warmth of one another's body and knew what it was. It was the warmth of life. Not since I was a child have I ever felt it again.

MARIE [*pulls loose*]: Listen, I'm not Marion.

DESIREE [*smiles*]: Why not stay a child all one's life? [*Embraces* MARIE *again.*] Then you wouldn't be Marie, but my adorable little Marion.

MARIE: You miss your childhood?

DESIREE: The gentleness, the warmth, even the padded quilt we slept under.

MARIE [*pulling loose*]: Not me. The present is enough for me. [*Goes back to work.*]

DESIREE: Why are you drudging away like this?

MARIE: I want to celebrate my graduation in a really spotless room. You get your doctor's degree only once in your life. Student life is over—now things get serious.

DESIREE: Words. Don't kid yourself.

MARIE: If you live by them, they're more than just words.

SCENE 3

[LUCY *enters.*]

LUCY: I can help you now.

MARIE: Clean water for the windows and the mirror, please.

[LUCY *exits with the bucket.*]

DESIREE [*laughs*]: Exchange of glances with the rival.

MARIE: Give me a break.

DESIREE: Did you see the way she looked at me?

[LUCY *returns with the bucket.*]

LUCY: Here's the clean water.

MARIE: Thank you, my dear.

DESIREE: Is Herr Freder coming today?

[LUCY *looks at her in fear and is silent.*]

DESIREE: I'm just asking.

MARIE: The room will be spic-and-span, right?

LUCY [*dully*]: Yes.

DESIREE: You're a pretty girl.

[LUCY *stares.*]

MARIE: Make sure, Lucy, that everything sparkles today.

DESIREE: I'm serious, you have very pretty eyes.

MARIE: The only thing missing is music.

DESIREE: Somebody might fall in love with you, Fräulein Lucy.

MARIE: A bachelorette party absolutely has to have music.

LUCY [*hurriedly*]: The gentleman in number 9 is away. He has a gramophone. I'll go and get it.

MARIE: You're an angel.

[LUCY *exits rapidly.*]

DESIREE [*shouting after her*]: Be brave, Lucy. I'm your friend. —Poor dumb animal.

MARIE [*washing the mirror*]: Go on. What happens to the larger caverns?

DESIREE [*reading again from notes*]: The larger caverns complicate the diagnosis because they may be a reservoir of pus. [*Sets down notes.*] Did you see her limp?

MARIE: Symptoms?

DESIREE [*reading again from notes*]: The symptoms of caverns, which almost never occur at the same time, are (a) percussion, (1) tympanatic ring, (2) metallic sound.

MARIE: Metallic sound when?

DESIREE: Only when the wall of the cavern is smooth and taut.

MARIE: Top marks.

[DESIREE *yawns.*]

MARIE: Too much talent is a disease. You should cram a little for the fun of it.

DESIREE: If I could run away from the classroom as simply as I ran away from home at seventeen, it wouldn't be so hard to take. If there were in the classroom a strict papa waiting to horsewhip me. And a kind, sad, helpless mama, who bursts into tears when

I disobey and then puts on a pearl necklace because she's off to a ball. If I could live that over again. Childhood is the only reason for living.

MARIE: I wouldn't want to relive my childhood. My parents hated one another.

DESIREE: So did mine. But, Marion, when you're little, you think it's funny. You figure it out later. When human beings hit seventeen, they should blow out their brains.

[MARIE *laughs.*]

DESIREE: After that, it's nothing but disappointments. To avoid them, I ran away. In silk stockings and a light wrap, and without a penny. [*Pauses.*]

[*Meanwhile,* MARIE *is working on a dress.*]

DESIREE: Your studies, your room, your dress, your lovers—you do it all yourself. Why try so hard?

MARIE: What you find superfluous, I find beautiful. That's the difference between us.

SCENE 4

[LUCY *enters with a letter.*]

LUCY: A gentleman. He's waiting outside.

DESIREE: You understand what I mean, Lucy? You're very pretty. Don't let anyone get the better of you.

MARIE [*perusing the letter*]: Quick. I wouldn't want Boysie to run into him.

[MARIE *exits with* LUCY.]

DESIREE [*taking the letter*]: A bill. Little Marion is deep in debt. [*Goes into her room to get some banknotes and slips them rapidly into the envelope.*]

MARIE [*returns, happily*]: I got rid of him. I gave Boysie a rococo writing desk. He says he'll write much more beautiful things on an antique desk. Inspiration, you understand . . .

DESIREE [*laughs*]: You're an idiot.

MARIE [*about to throw away the envelope, she discovers the banknotes; looks at* DESIREE *in surprise*]: Was this you?

DESIREE [*arms around* MARIE*'s neck*]: My little Marion.

MARIE: I won't take it.

DESIREE: Idiot. [*Kisses her.*] What? Because you're in love with a man? I have to keep an eye on you.

MARIE: You crazy child.

DESIREE: A child, like you, because I'm in love too. But with you.

MARIE: Let go of me.

DESIREE [*kisses her passionately*]: Only women can help each other out.

MARIE: Let go of me.

DESIREE [*with a wild laugh*]: I won't let go of you. I won't let go of you. If you promise me—

MARIE [*pushes her away; pauses*]: Let's not mention it again.

DESIREE [*turning pale*]: Marion.

MARIE: Poor devil. [*She sits; begins to sew again.*] So the symptoms of percussion: (2) metallic sound, (3) . . . ?

[DESIREE *looks at* MARIE, *then turns to the door to her room.*]

MARIE: Your money, Daisy.

[DESIREE *takes the money and her book, goes into her room*.]

MARIE [*watches her leave; pauses; goes to the door*]: Shame on you, you silly child. [*Tries to open it.*] Open up. I didn't mean to hurt you. Open up, Daisy.

SCENE 5

[FREDER *enters.*]

MARIE [*nervously*]: You?

FREDER: I have to see Daisy. The door on the other side is locked.

MARIE: This one too.

FREDER: Ah?

MARIE: You talk about things that are none of your business.

[FREDER *observes her.*]

MARIE [*nervously*]: I've never enjoyed having you around. I have to be frank, Herr Freder. [*She folds the dress.*]

FREDER: The party dress?

[MARIE *doesn't answer.*]

FREDER: Congratulations.

[MARIE *doesn't answer.*]

FREDER: You've managed to do in ten semesters what it took me twenty-five to do. Hurray for you. A superwoman, alias *Terminus technicus*. And not unlike me.

[MARIE *stares at him.*]

[FREDER *stands and laughs.*]

MARIE [*carefully*]: An athlete.

FREDER [*laughs*]: "Where are the twentieth-century barbarians?" asks Nietzsche. And quite right too. Here I stand before you.

MARIE: You could exhibit yourself in a freak show.

[FREDER *laughs even louder.*]

MARIE: Go to hell.

FREDER: You'll be calling for me, sooner or later.

MARIE: You're drunk this early in the morning.

FREDER: And why not?

MARIE: An athlete.

FREDER: People can't do without me that easily. Ask Daisy.

MARIE: She despises you.

FREDER [*friendly*]: Not in bed, my angel.

MARIE: How dare you?

FREDER: First let darling Irene get her hooks into Boysie.

MARIE: Irene?

FREDER: That sterile little sow.

MARIE: What makes you think you can call Herr Petrell "Boysie"?

FREDER: I find him very attractive.

MARIE: Nobody asked you.

FREDER: A gentle dreamer, an adorable incompetent. When it comes to sex, he appeals to every woman's maternal instinct.

MARIE: Anything else?

FREDER: I'm open to anything. [*Pulls a bottle of cognac out of his pocket.*] Congratulations.

MARIE [*nervous*]: That wasn't necessary.

FREDER: Indeed. Why do we need doctors at all in this decadent age? The more disease there is, the more pointless the medics. But you still drudge away to save Baby Boy Blue's skin. And your own. There's a better remedy for despair than working.

MARIE: You can be sure I'll follow your example.

FREDER: You'll enjoy it.

MARIE: You're wrong.

FREDER: Anyone who celebrates a graduation—

MARIE: I want no gifts.

FREDER: You want no gifts from me.

[MARIE *is silent.*]

FREDER: I'll invite myself.

MARIE: We're not planning a party.

FREDER: All the better.

MARIE: You're very intrusive.

FREDER: You're very impolite, my fair lady.

MARIE: Perhaps.

FREDER: Why can't you stand me?

MARIE: You're right about that.

FREDER: It's, how shall I put it, dangerous.

[MARIE *laughs.*]

FREDER: Dangerous to hate a man so much.

MARIE: I don't hate you.

FREDER: That remains to be seen.

MARIE: You are very conceited.

FREDER [*laughs*]: For good reason.

SCENE 6

[DESIREE *enters, wearing a hat.*]

MARIE [*quickly*]: I'll walk you as far as the college. [*She puts on her hat.*]

[DESIREE *smiles at* FREDER.]

FREDER [*laughs*]: Her ladyship has an exam today?

DESIREE: You seem to be better.

FREDER: Give me your hand.

MARIE: I'll get my jacket.

DESIREE: He reeks of alcohol first thing in the morning.

FREDER: You stood me up.

DESIREE: The woman to console you is not far away.

FREDER: The consolation isn't worth a damn.

DESIREE: You miss me a little?

FREDER: No man can forget you.

MARIE [*impatient, to* FREDER]: Are you coming with us?

DESIREE [*laughs*]: For heaven's sake.

[DESIREE *exits rapidly.*]

[MARIE *follows her.*]

SCENE 7

[LUCY *enters.*]

FREDER [*calmly*]: Lucy.

LUCY [*stands in place*]: I have to take the water away.

FREDER: What water?

LUCY [*points at the bucket*]: That there, Herr Freder.

FREDER: Liar. [*Sits to one side.*] When you come for a bucket, you don't creep in. Come over here. What did you want?

LUCY [*anxious and confused*]: Herr Freder.

FREDER: Shall I tell you?

LUCY: You're hurting me.

FREDER: Where? I'm not touching you.

[LUCY *is silent.*]

FREDER: Where am I hurting you?

[LUCY *weeps.*]

FREDER: When you saw the two of them go out, you wanted a moment alone with me?

LUCY [*quietly*]: Yes.

FREDER: You should have the courage to take what you want. Not the bucket of water, that's a lie, but . . .

LUCY: You're hurting me.

FREDER: Where, damn it? I'm not even touching you.

[LUCY *slowly starts to sob.*]

FREDER [*more gently*]: There, there, you're a good girl.

LUCY [*stares at him and moves toward him*]: Herr Freder.

FREDER [*stroking her hair*]: A good girl. [*He draws her to him, pats her on the back.*] You're my little bitch.

LUCY: Yes.

FREDER: My little beastie.

LUCY: Yes. Yes.

FREDER [*lifts her head*]: Look me in the face. [*Pauses.*] Bright eyes, lovely eyes.

LUCY [*quietly*]: Yes.

FREDER [*kisses her eyes*]: Did anyone ever tell you that?

LUCY [*quietly*]: No.

FREDER: Were you able to sleep last night?

[LUCY *shakes her head no.*]

FREDER: Why not?

LUCY [*smiles*]: Herr Freder.

FREDER [*strokes her hair*]: Love me?

LUCY [*smiles*]: Don't ask.

[FREDER *draws her to him.*]

LUCY [*unresisting*]: Herr Freder.

FREDER [*kisses her*]: Dear little girl.

LUCY [*unresisting*]: What if someone comes?

FREDER: I love you.

LUCY [*kisses his hands, almost in tears*]: Ah.

FREDER: Well, say something.

LUCY: I can't.

FREDER [*quietly*]: And this morning?

[LUCY *nods.*]

FREDER: Speak.

LUCY: I can't.

FREDER: You pulled it off?

[LUCY *nods.*]

FREDER: What?

LUCY [*quietly*]: Two rings.

FREDER: From Frau Schimmelbrot?

[LUCY *nods.*]

FREDER: She was still asleep?

[LUCY *nods.*]

FREDER: You're sure she didn't notice anything?

LUCY: Not a thing.

FREDER: Tell me.

LUCY: I can't.

FREDER: Where were the rings?

LUCY: In the dresser. The second drawer.

FREDER: You knew it already?

LUCY: That's where she always hides her jewels.

FREDER: You lit a candle?

LUCY: It was almost daylight.

FREDER: It was daylight already?

LUCY: There was light enough through the gaps in the blinds.

FREDER: You moved to the bed first?

LUCY: The way you told me to.

FREDER: How close?

LUCY: Up to the night table.

FREDER: What was on the night table?

LUCY: A glass of water and hairpins.

FREDER: Frau Schimmelbrot's?

[LUCY *nods.*]

FREDER: This kind of hairpin? [*He loosens her hair.*]

LUCY [*unresisting*]: Herr Freder.

FREDER [*kisses her hair*]: What an aroma.

LUCY: What if someone comes?

FREDER: Look me in the face. Lovely eyes. [*He kisses her eyes.*]

LUCY: Herr Freder.

FREDER: Where are the rings?

LUCY: Under my pillow.

FREDER: Someone might find them there.

LUCY [*frightened*]: You want me to bring them to you?

FREDER: Hide them in the dining room.

[LUCY *nods.*]

FREDER: Under the sideboard.

[LUCY *nods*.]

FREDER: Now get up.

[LUCY *pulls loose from* FREDER.]

FREDER: Tonight I'll come up to your room.

LUCY [*panting*]: Yes.

FREDER: We'll make love again.

LUCY: Yes.

FREDER: What kind of rings?

LUCY: I didn't look at them.

FREDER: Gold?

LUCY: I don't know.

FREDER: Frau Schimmelbrot didn't notice anything?

LUCY: She's still asleep.

FREDER: But suppose she notices?

LUCY: She rarely puts on her rings.

FREDER: One day she's bound to notice they're gone.

LUCY [*indifferently*]: I don't know. [*Suddenly*] Nobody will suspect you.

FREDER: What's it got to do with me?

LUCY [*quickly*]: Nothing. And even if they kill me, nobody will know about you.

FREDER: Why the hell bring me into it? You're the one who wanted to do it.

LUCY: I'm the only one who wanted to do it.

FREDER: What's it got to do with me? Fix your hair.

[LUCY *does so.*]

FREDER: I want to help you.

LUCY: Herr Freder.

[FREDER *embraces her.*]

LUCY [*unresisting*]: What if someone comes?

FREDER: Frau Schimmelbrot, I suppose.

LUCY: Herr Freder.

FREDER: Why are you trembling?

LUCY: I'm not afraid for my sake.

FREDER [*letting go of her*]: We shall see.

LUCY: I'm not afraid for my sake.

FREDER: Didn't you come to take away the water?

LUCY: What water?

FREDER [*pointing to the bucket*]: There.

LUCY [*not moving*]: Yes.

FREDER: Take it away.

LUCY [*not moving*]: Yes.

FREDER: And the rings.

LUCY [*awakes*]: Yes. Under the sideboard.

FREDER: So I don't have to look for them too long.

LUCY: Under the carpet, near the right foot.

FREDER: Under the carpet, near the right foot. Take away the bucket.

[LUCY *takes the bucket.*]

FREDER: Make it snappy!

LUCY: Herr Freder.

FREDER: Is it too heavy?

LUCY: No.

FREDER: Am I supposed to help you?

LUCY [*quickly*]: No.

FREDER [*heading for* DESIREE*'s door*]: I'm going to lie down in here.

LUCY [*frightened*]: Yes.

FREDER: Might you be jealous?

[LUCY *is silent.*]

FREDER: Of Desiree? Don't forget that she's a countess.

LUCY [*vehemently*]: Who ran away from home.

FREDER [*laugh*]: True enough.

LUCY: At seventeen she'd already—

FREDER: What about you?

[LUCY *is silent.*]

FREDER: Then shut up.

LUCY: Every night, she goes to bed—

FREDER: Don't splash that water all over the place.

LUCY: I hate her. I'd rather be—

FREDER: Shut your trap.

LUCY: Herr Freder.

FREDER: I'm going to lie down. [*He goes into* DESIREE's *room.*]

LUCY [*quietly*]: Herr Freder.

SCENE 8

[IRENE *and* PETRELL *enter.*]

PETRELL: Anyone here?

LUCY: The young lady has exams today.

[LUCY *exits.*]

IRENE [*laughs*]: Desiree and her exams.

PETRELL [*stretching*]: Marie must have gone with her.

IRENE: Make yourself comfortable, Herr Boysie.

[PETRELL *laughs.*]

IRENE: That's Marie's nickname for you.

PETRELL: For Marie I'm a plaything.

IRENE: We all are, Herr Boysie.

PETRELL: Stop that.

IRENE: Are you capable of reacting?

PETRELL: Outside just now, it was getting on my nerves.

IRENE: I won't say it any more. Then, too, everything she does is vain and pointless.

PETRELL: Who?

IRENE: Desiree. A dilettante.

PETRELL: Even though she was taught by a totally idiotic tutor, she got her diploma at first try.

IRENE: Thanks to Alt—he was the one who spent nights cramming with her.

PETRELL: Even today, she passes every exam with honors.

IRENE: Because she's a countess. But she has no idea of the meaning of work.

PETRELL: Don't get excited.

IRENE: Those of us who had to claw our way up, nobody notices us, we're left in the shadows. In science it's the same thing—the daredevil triumphs, never the worker.

PETRELL: The creative person is always a daredevil.

[IRENE *laughs*.]

PETRELL: Go on, it suits you splendidly.

IRENE: Now she's two semesters ahead of me. But we'll see who'll be the first to finish her thesis. Ah, why do I bother with her?

PETRELL: Don't get excited.

IRENE: Nothing but bluff. What's really on her mind, we know. I have more respect for any streetwalker—at least she talks honestly about what she does.

PETRELL: So you want to be a doctor?

IRENE: I won't let a countess's coronet put me off my game. Anyway, she'll come to a bad end.

PETRELL: Who will?

IRENE: Desiree.

PETRELL [*nods*]: Now you're talking sense.

IRENE: You're mistaken, I have no pity. She should have stayed at home, safe and sound, with her papa the count.

PETRELL: What does your father do?

IRENE: You're off topic.

PETRELL [*laughs*]: What is the topic?

IRENE: We'll talk about it again next year.

PETRELL: Next year—

IRENE: When Desiree has gone the way of all depressed harlots. She'll end up in an opium den.

PETRELL [*laughs*]: For heaven's sake.

IRENE: Or the morgue.

PETRELL [*closer*]: Why are you always so bitter?

IRENE: Actually, I don't care.

PETRELL: Really.

IRENE: I'm nobody's fool, that's all.

PETRELL: Do you envy her because of her men?

IRENE [*malicious laugh*]: Freder, perhaps?

PETRELL: How old are you? You're very young. You're very pretty. Why do you always show your claws?

IRENE [*laughs*]: Stop.

PETRELL: You really are very pretty. But no one dares to tell you.

IRENE: It's easier with Desiree.

PETRELL: What are you trying to do?

IRENE: I take my career seriously, that's all. A woman who studies cannot play the whore at the same time. That's a blot on science.

PETRELL: Science is the immaculate conception.

IRENE: Boysie.

PETRELL: Does having no one make you immaculate?

[IRENE *doesn't answer.*]

PETRELL: You aren't with anyone?

IRENE: Science demands total commitment. Absolute solitude.

PETRELL: Words.

IRENE [*smiles*]: Boysie . . . !

PETRELL: Call me Boysie, for all I care. It's something else. It's inhibitions.

IRENE: Don't be silly.

PETRELL: That inferiority complex of yours. Every decent person feels inferior deep inside. You've got to fight it. You have a reputation for being proud and inaccessible. But your pride is nothing but repressed anxiety, shyness, fear of other people.

IRENE [*laughs*]: Write a short story about it.

PETRELL: If a man dared to touch you—you'd kill him. You've never had a man, have you?

[IRENE *is silent.*]

PETRELL: I don't believe in unfeeling natures: you're afraid, plain and simple.

IRENE: Will you shut up?

PETRELL: When a beautiful woman lets a man stroke her hair, it doesn't mean she's a slut.

IRENE: Put it all in writing. You can use it. For your new rococo desk.

PETRELL [*stands beside her*]: Why are you always so sarcastic?

IRENE: Because I find it all laughable.

PETRELL [*cautiously strokes her hair*]: You are beautiful, Irene.

IRENE [*motionless*]: Stop playing around.

PETRELL [*hesitant*]: I'm not playing.

IRENE: Take your hand away.

PETRELL: I don't want to. [*He embraces her.*]

IRENE [*motionless*]: Boysie.

PETRELL: A little girl punishing herself.

IRENE [*quietly*]: Let go of me. Think of Marie.

PETRELL [*smiles*]: Marie can't see us. [*He suddenly draws her to him and kisses her.*]

IRENE [*tries to pull loose*]: Herr Petrell.

PETRELL: Cheat. You're capable of any vice.

IRENE [*pulled loose*]: I don't want any stolen love.

PETRELL: Words.

IRENE: You're taking advantage of our being alone.

PETRELL: The only thing you've left out is: Yech!

IRENE: You don't know me at all.

PETRELL: Let me know you better.

IRENE: First ask Marie's permission.

PETRELL: What a beast you are.

IRENE: She defends her cub like a she-lion. Don't provoke her.

PETRELL: I'm not her son.

IRENE [*laughs*]: Boysie.

PETRELL: I'm not her son.

IRENE [*laughs*]: Boysie.

PETRELL: I'm a free man and can do whatever I want.

IRENE [*laughs*]: Boysie.

PETRELL: Don't tempt me.

IRENE: Sit down at that rococo desk your mother bought you so your brilliant ideas won't run away.

PETRELL: Stop.

IRENE [*laughing harder and harder*]: This association of mental effort with a piece of furniture—it could make you sick. The kind of mentality that's infiltrating science today. A depressed harlot and an ambitious farm girl from Passau.

PETRELL: You're jealous of Marie as well? I feel sorry for you.

IRENE: I'm not talking about you. With a good, rigorous education, you might have made something of yourself.

PETRELL: I'm not ambitious.

IRENE: Liar. The things you write are dreadful. Even if five lines sometimes show a sign of individual talent. It's a shame.

PETRELL: You read my writing so attentively?

IRENE: It's a shame about you.

PETRELL: I'm not so old.

IRENE: You might achieve power and fame.

PETRELL [*ironically*]: Power and fame.

IRENE: Go on, laugh. In reality, this secret ambition devours everyone who works with his mind.

PETRELL: I'm not devoured.

IRENE: You're nothing at all. You're still at your mother's breast. What do you know of the satisfaction that comes from painful nights of solitude, despair in work, your girlfriend's mama's boy?

PETRELL: Are you speaking seriously or sneering at me?

IRENE: As seriously as I can. [*She stares at him.*]

PETRELL [*after a pause*]: As seriously as you can?

IRENE [*quietly*]: Yes.

PETRELL: Irene.

IRENE: Don't touch me.

PETRELL: You confuse me.

IRENE: Poor little boy. [*She laughs.*] Keep your hands to yourself. You feel obliged to throw yourself at every woman you think wishes you well?

PETRELL: You wish me well?

IRENE [*suddenly*]: There's someone in the other room.

PETRELL [*opens* DESIREE'*s door*]: Herr Freder.

IRENE [*frightened*]: Herr Freder?

FREDER [*from the room*]: Come in, Petrell.

PETRELL: Fräulein Irene is here. Don't let us disturb you. [*Closes the door.*]

IRENE [*quickly*]: He heard us.

PETRELL: He's lying on the sofa by the far wall.

IRENE: Don't trust him.

PETRELL: You'd like me to distrust everybody.

IRENE: I have my head on straight.

PETRELL: That's how you destroy every one of life's pleasures.

IRENE [*laughs*]: Pleasures.

PETRELL: A foreign word, eh?

IRENE: Solitude to the point of despair. When it produces something, that's the only pleasure.

PETRELL: Puritan.

IRENE: We really don't understand one another. How long have you known Marie?

PETRELL: Two years.

IRENE: At the time, you were—

PETRELL: —a student at the university, one of those who hated science. Marie made my life beautiful. I owe her a great deal.

IRENE [*scornful*]: At least you're grateful.

PETRELL: If it weren't for her, I would have starved to death, literally starved to death.

IRENE: At your mother's breast . . .

PETRELL [*beside himself*]: You are horrible.

IRENE: Every rational person is horrible in another person's eyes because the rational person sees through him. Today you wouldn't be here if Marie hadn't—

PETRELL: I would have starved to death.

IRENE: Nobody starves to death. Just before dying, you come to and realize who you are. I had no mother's breast, and I didn't starve to death.

PETRELL: You've led a dog's life.

IRENE [*laughing*]: Thank God.

PETRELL: I don't envy you.

IRENE: That's why I am invincible.

SCENE 9

[FREDER *comes out of* DESIREE'*s room.*]

FREDER [*laughs*]: Is a plot afoot?

[IRENE *picks up a book.*]

PETRELL: We're waiting for Marie.

FREDER: More than likely.

[PETRELL *stretches out.*]

FREDER: Have you had a close look at that room?

PETRELL: No.

FREDER: Spic-and-span top to bottom. This graduation is turning into a real birthday party.

PETRELL: Don't spoil her fun.

FREDER: Health, happiness and a long life.

PETRELL: Cheers.

FREDER: Your Marie was born under a lucky star.

PETRELL: Science will tell you there's no such thing as health.

FREDER: Science is reading a new book. Do not disturb.

IRENE: I'm not talking to you. [*She goes on reading.*]

FREDER: Yet it was your voice just now that woke me up.

IRENE: I've long suspected you were eavesdropping.

FREDER: And looking through keyholes.

PETRELL [*anxious*]: Is that true?

FREDER [*looks at him*]: Absolutely.

IRENE [*quickly*]: We have nothing to hide.

FREDER: Nothing I don't already know.

IRENE [*laughs*]: Don't let yourself be intimidated, Herr Petrell.

FREDER: Boysie.

PETRELL: What do you mean, "Boysie"?

FREDER: Girlsie.

IRENE: You're drunk. [*She goes on reading.*]

FREDER: Weren't you playing Boysie-Girlsie?

IRENE [*rises*]: Will you see me out, Herr Petrell?

FREDER: A pretty young man, this Boysie.

PETRELL [*rises*]: We should wait for Marie.

IRENE: We can do it downstairs.

FREDER [*laughs*]: What would she think?

IRENE: That your presence chased us out.

FREDER: But Girlsie.

IRENE: Come on.

PETRELL: Stop this idiocy.

FREDER: I'll wait for Desiree.

IRENE: Desiree's room is next door.

FREDER: Tell me something I don't know.

IRENE: This is absurd. [*They sit down again.*]

FREDER [*pauses*]: What're you reading? [*He stretches out.*]

[IRENE *does not reply.*]

FREDER: Come and sit beside me, Petrell. I took your seat.

PETRELL: Stay, stay.

FREDER: If only she weren't so mean.

PETRELL: Don't provoke her.

FREDER: Such a pretty girl.

IRENE: Keep your tastelessness to yourself.

FREDER [*laughs*]: Back again?

PETRELL: Will Marie wait till the exam is over?

FREDER: I doubt it.

IRENE: I'm telling you, Petrell—Desiree will pass with honors.

FREDER: Desiree passes with honors in all sorts of exams.

IRENE [*sneering*]: You ought to know.

FREDER: She excels in whatever she does.

IRENE: Spare us the details.

FREDER [*laughs*]: Now you're the one being tasteless.

[IRENE *reads.*]

FREDER: What are you going to give Marie?

PETRELL: I haven't had enough time.

FREDER [*showing the bottle of cognac*]: My gift.

PETRELL: Marie doesn't drink.

FREDER: Boysie will have to overcome her principles.

IRENE: Meanwhile, she's instilling them in him.

FREDER: We agree there, Girlsie.

IRENE: Shut up.

PETRELL: In fact, Marie is so basically healthy . . .

IRENE: What is that supposed to mean?

FREDER: Bravo. There's no such thing as health.

IRENE: Youth in any case is never healthy. The mind is dormant in a dream.

PETRELL [*quietly*]: Youth is dormant in a dream. That's beautiful, Irene.

IRENE: You're beguiling yourself with words. Youth is a dangerous place to stay. Youth is latent proximity to death.

PETRELL: Youth is the only adventure in our life.

FREDER: You interrupt her only to say the same thing.

IRENE: Adapted for the rococo desk.

PETRELL: Irene.

IRENE [*quickly*]: I beg your pardon.

PETRELL: You know that magnificent saying of Novalis: "Nothing distinguishes man from nature so much as his obsessive love for pain and disease."

IRENE: Novalis was a neurotic.

PETRELL [*exalted*]: His obsessive love! We are obsessed!

FREDER: You're in love with words.

IRENE: He's a poet.

FREDER [*smoking*]: I'm conducting an interesting experiment.

PETRELL [*quietly*]: Poet? I don't know that I'm a poet.

FREDER: I'm conducting an interesting experiment. I am persuading someone to commit a theft on my behalf.

PETRELL: You're a menace to society.

FREDER: All science is a menace to society.

IRENE: You're not a scientist.

PETRELL: We won't know that till much later.

IRENE [*upset*]: I consider you . . .

FREDER [*straightens up*]: Go on, say it.

IRENE: Better not.

FREDER: Courage, Girlsie.

IRENE: I think you have a criminal nature.

FREDER [*laughs*]: It goes with the job.

IRENE: But you have no job.

FREDER: You're upset because you're afraid of me.

IRENE: You have delusions of grandeur.

FREDER: Afraid. You suspect that mine is the only way. To be creative means to be in danger. Not only in theory, Girlsie. Science doesn't mean thumbing through textbooks with a wet finger. But you know all about it and you distrust it.

IRENE: You're what I distrust—someday you'll go to prison.

FREDER: Any really great man belongs in prison.

IRENE: Ridiculous.

FREDER: You cling desperately to your books because your instinct puts you on guard against reality. In fact, you know it perfectly. Congratulations, you're pretty and smart.

IRENE [*leaps up*]: I can't stand listening to this any longer.

FREDER [*to* PETRELL]: I've already seduced her halfway.

IRENE [*furious*]: Leave that boy alone.

FREDER [*laughs*]: Boysie.

IRENE: Nothing's sacred to you.

FREDER: Boysie could be corrupted.

PETRELL: Corrupted?

IRENE: Don't listen to him!

FREDER: Don't listen, Boysie.

IRENE: I won't listen either.

FREDER: Now you're lying.

[IRENE *turns away from him.*]

FREDER: Shall I tell you about my experiment?

IRENE: We don't want to become accomplices to your crimes.

FREDER: Tonight, at 11:00, when no one will see us?

PETRELL: Why are you provoking her?

FREDER: Just the two of us, strictly scientific.

IRENE: Don't answer him.

PETRELL: You are being cruel.

FREDER: I'm doing research.

PETRELL: At this moment too?

FREDER: Surprised, Boysie, eh?

IRENE: Absurd, all of it.

FREDER: "In science too, nothing can ever be truly *known* unless it is *acted upon.*"

IRENE: Absurd.

FREDER [*laughs*]: So says Goethe.

PETRELL [*surprised*]: Goethe?

FREDER: He wrote more than "The Elf King." But perhaps Boysie isn't supposed to know that?

IRENE [*to* PETRELL]: You want to stay here any longer?

FREDER: Don't put on an act, my pigeon. You can defend your-self perfectly well without that. You are the healthiest of us all. Healthier than strapping Marie. But you—you know the dangers, that's the big difference.

PETRELL: Let's talk about something else.

FREDER: Quiet, she loves listening to this. Anyone who lets the limits of the law impose on the limits of science ends up a musty old cabinet minister. You, Fräulein, are bound to be a cabinet minister.

PETRELL: That'll do.

FREDER: I won't even be a doctor.

PETRELL: Take your time.

FREDER: Twenty-four semesters.

PETRELL: How romantic, the perennial student.

FREDER: You're an idiot. I beg your pardon.

PETRELL [*laughs*]: Don't mention it.

FREDER: If I were a woman, I might fall in love with you too, same as Girlsie.

PETRELL: Fräulein Irene is not in love with me.

FREDER: This is not for your ears, Boysie. Your childish innocence would plunge any woman into the most delectable folly. You seem to know that. Has Daisy never been in love with you?

[IRENE *pricks up her ears.*]

PETRELL: Never.

FREDER: I'm not jealous.

PETRELL: Never, honestly.

FREDER: You could awaken maternal feelings even in Daisy.

SCENE 10

[ALT *enters.*]

[FREDER *stretches out again.*]

ALT: The girl graduate isn't here?

PETRELL: Desiree has an exam today.

FREDER: Petrell, let me have a cigarette.

ALT [*quietly*]: So it's true?

IRENE [*anxious*]: What?

ALT: Better watch out.

IRENE [*laughs*]: I don't understand.

FREDER [*to* PETRELL]: It's about me. Desiree—

PETRELL: You want me to swear to you?

FREDER: Women seem to fall for you.

PETRELL: Desiree barely looks my way.

FREDER: She's had too many bad experiences with tender teenagers.

ALT: I won't let it happen.

IRENE: You're dreaming.

ALT: She'll find out about it.

IRENE: I'm not going to be frightened by a country girl.

FREDER: You love to play the skeptic, but you're not one.

PETRELL: With you, one never knows what to think.

FREDER: That's your feminine weapon. [*Indicating* IRENE.] Girlsie's feminine weapon is pride.

PETRELL: Don't call her Girlsie.

FREDER [*laughs*]: You drop your illusions pretty quickly.

PETRELL: What are you getting at?

FREDER: You live on words. You can't call Girlsie an ideal.

PETRELL Anyway, it's none of your business.

ALT: You didn't have to go up to his room.

IRENE: I pity the man with a dirty mind.

ALT: What were you doing at his place so early in the morning?

IRENE [*laughs*]: I wanted to admire the rococo writing desk.

FREDER: Marie's feminine weapon is her robust health. Some people resist by disarmament. When it comes down to it, we're all the same. All poor bastards.

PETRELL: I'd really like to go home.

FREDER: To work.

PETRELL: Right again.

FREDER: The new desk.

PETRELL: You're making fun of me again.

FREDER: Little things inspire great projects. But perseverance is something else again.

PETRELL: I'd like to write a great novel.

FREDER: You're very inspired at the moment.

PETRELL: You'll have the leading role.

[FREDER *laughs*.]

IRENE: I wasn't there more than three minutes, long enough to collect him.

ALT: And now you're overcome with scruples.

IRENE: If behind every harmless—

ALT: It wasn't harmless.

IRENE: You think that—

ALT: There was nothing harmless about the intention.

IRENE: I feel sorry for you.

SCENE 11

MARIE [*enters.*]

MARIE: Alt? How nice. [*She removes her hat and coat.*]

ALT: Three cheers.

FREDER: Hip, hip, hurray.

PETRELL [*quietly*]: Now I know.

IRENE: What?

PETRELL: Freder told me.

IRENE: Keep quiet.

PETRELL: You're in love with me.

IRENE: Keep quiet—not here.

ALT: Where's Desiree holed up?

IRENE: With top grades, naturally?

MARIE: We were together only as far as the gate.

FREDER: For her, failure would finally be a blessed event.

MARIE: What do you say, Boysie? [*She goes to* PETRELL.]

IRENE: You've got Desiree on your conscience.

ALT: Everyone must have something.

IRENE: People don't go to the operating theater in silk stockings.

FREDER: Why not?

PETRELL: By the way, thank you for the desk.

MARIE: When did it get here?

PETRELL: This morning. I was still asleep.

MARIE: It's beautiful, isn't it?

PETRELL: Very beautiful. They had to wake me up.

MARIE: Are you pleased?

PETRELL: Too beautiful, perhaps.

MARIE: You'll get used to it soon enough.

PETRELL: Yes.

MARIE: Are you worried? About where you're going to put it?

PETRELL: In my bedroom.

MARIE [*laughs*]: I should have guessed! Tell me.

PETRELL: What?

MARIE: Why are you so grumpy?

PETRELL: Doesn't matter.

MARIE: Go on, tell me.

PETRELL [*vehemently*]: Don't question me like that.

MARIE: You're being silly.

PETRELL: You're starting to remind me of my mother.

MARIE [*laughs*]: Do I, sonny boy?

PETRELL: One mother is enough for me.

MARIE: Naughty, naughty, Boysie.

PETRELL: A mama's boy for her lover—that's too much.

IRENE [*having listened attentively*]: Are we in the way?

PETRELL: Where'd you get that idea?

IRENE: We can go somewhere else.

FREDER [*erupts*]: Thalassa! Thalassa!

IRENE: What did you say?

FREDER: Thalassa! Thalassa!

ALT: Let him have his fun.

FREDER: It's the Greek war cry. Didn't you go to high school?

IRENE: You're very witty.

FREDER: The battle begins.

IRENE: *Delirium tremens.*

FREDER: Form up, 'ten-shun, Boysie front and center.

MARIE: Stop this nonsense.

FREDER: Forward march, Girlsie. We'd like to be around to see it.

MARIE [*laughs*]: Who's Girlsie?

FREDER: Fräulein Irene.

IRENE: Be quiet.

FREDER: May I introduce Boysie's Girlsie? [*He whistles.*]

ALT [*holds* IRENE *back*]: She's going for your face.

FREDER [*whistles*]: Go ahead.

[MARIE *heads for* FREDER.]

FREDER: Calm down, golden girl.

MARIE: You wouldn't dare.

FREDER: Keep an eye on your little darling.

MARIE: Get out.

FREDER: Or give him up. [*Suddenly embraces* MARIE.] He isn't right for you.

MARIE [*quickly pulling loose*]: You boor.

FREDER: A pat on the bottom for this sterile skeleton.

IRENE: I don't have to put up with this.

[IRENE *quickly exits.*]

FREDER [*laughs*]: Put up with it, and how.

MARIE: What's that about?

PETRELL: We should bring her back.

[PETRELL *quickly exits.*]

MARIE [*nonplussed*]: No.

[FREDER *goes on whistling.*]

MARIE: What's going on?

[MARIE *exits.*]

ALT: You've engineered a disaster.

FREDER [*looks at him; after a pause*]: Herr Alt, she finds you far more attractive.

[FREDER *exits.*]

[MARIE *enters quickly.*]

MARIE: They're downstairs already. [*She takes her jacket and hat.*]

ALT: Two steps at a time.

MARIE [*laughs*]: Can you can explain what's going on?

ALT: Where are you going?

MARIE: I want to catch up to them.

ALT [*stung*]: Don't bother. Come and sit next to me.

[MARIE *looks at him in astonishment.*]

ALT: Over here, Marie.

MARIE: I don't understand you.

ALT: Let them run.

MARIE: But they're not running. Not in the street.

ALT: Maybe they are running, even in the street.

[MARIE *loses her energy.*]

ALT: Come and sit down.

[MARIE *doesn't move.*]

ALT: Take off your hat.

[MARIE *does so mechanically.*]

ALT: The jacket too.

MARIE [*sits down; after a pause*]: You're imagining things.

ALT: Make yourself comfortable. We have plenty of time.

MARIE [*laughs*]: No, we don't, my dear. She doesn't matter enough for that.

ALT: It's never the things that matter that lay us low.

MARIE: It isn't true, all that.

ALT: I lost my job at the general hospital, I've spent years in prison. A kid at death's door was in such pain that I cut short his agony. I gave him morphine instead of camphor. Are you listening?

MARIE: Morphine instead of camphor.

ALT: My life was snuffed out. And I would like to live it over again. You understand?

MARIE: You would like to live it over again.

ALT: I would like to live it over again.

MARIE: You would like to live it over again. [*She laughs.*] No, it isn't serious.

ALT: Nothing is serious to a little boy.

MARIE: And just like that, I should tear him out of my heart?

ALT: Sentenced for manslaughter, two years in prison. You would have done the same.

MARIE: What?

ALT: It clearly shows the obsolescence of the penal law.

MARIE: I'm going crazy.

ALT: The concepts we live by are obsolete. You should realize that. Do you hear me?

MARIE: I should realize that.

ALT: You should realize that.

MARIE: I should realize that. [*Laughs.*] He must be at her place by now.

ALT: Fists clenched.

MARIE [*mechanically*]: Fists clenched.

ALT: Come down to earth.

MARIE: Come down to earth.

ALT: Wake up. Clinging to other people is a weakness.

MARIE: To live like Freder is strength.

ALT: Fully self-conscious.

MARIE: Fully conscious. [*Laughs.*] Rhythmic gymnastics. We're both crazy.

ALT: Now you're coming to your senses.

MARIE: Now I'm coming to my senses.

ALT: Erase him from your memory.

MARIE: You're turning into an animal, like Freder.

ALT: Freder is not an animal.

MARIE: A criminal.

ALT: Aren't I one as well?

MARIE [*astonished*]: You. She's at his place.

ALT: His place.

MARIE: His place? [*She starts to laugh; the laugh quickly grows louder.*] And I was the one who smartened this up, barely an hour ago, and for whom? Laugh with me. Spic-and-span. [*She grabs the bottle in front of her and throws it against the mirror.*] Smithereens. You heard that crash? No more spic-and-span room—it's a shambles. We live in a shambles. Laugh with me.

ALT [*furious*]: I am laughing with you.

MARIE: We live in a shambles.

ALT: We live in a shambles.

MARIE: Up to now I've been dreaming. Idiot. Idiot. A shambles. Laugh with me. An idiot in a shambles. An idiot in a shambles. Ah, I don't hear you laughing. [*She faints.*]

[ALT *catches her and strokes her hair.*]

[*Curtain.*]

ACT II

[*Evening. Flowers in the room.*]

SCENE 1

[MARIE *and* DESIREE *dance to gramophone music.*]

DESIREE: Smaller steps.

MARIE [*laughs*]: I can't yet. Patience.

DESIREE: You can do anything.

MARIE: You're wooing me a little too obviously.

DESIREE: Marion.

[MARIE *laughs.*]

DESIREE: My own Marion.

MARIE [*laughs*]: Not yet.

DESIREE: Don't stiffen your back like that. The hips have to be more supple.

MARIE: Easy to say.

DESIREE: Cold showers, massage and Swedish gymnastics every morning.

MARIE: As if I had the time.

DESIREE: We'll make the time. Training spares you a thousand needless thoughts per hour. [*Laughs.*] You stepped on my foot.

MARIE: Again!

DESIREE: I can forgive you anything.

MARIE: You still love me?

DESIREE: Silly little girl.

MARIE [*stops dancing*]: How did it go?

DESIREE: What?

MARIE [*laughs*]: It was an inner victory. "It was an inner victory to break away from the grip of habit at long last."

DESIREE: You know that stupid letter by heart already.

MARIE: "To break away, escape from oneself like the prairie mustang from the locked corral."

DESIREE: You were the corral.

MARIE: "That bit of prairie within us . . ."

DESIREE: Stop.

MARIE: The corral was me.

DESIREE: And the prairie has red hair.

MARIE: May I read it to you? [*She looks for the letter.*]

DESIREE: For heaven's sake. [*She winds up the gramophone.*]

MARIE [*reads the letter*]: "It was an inner victory to break away from the grip of . . ."

DESIREE: Listen.

MARIE: ". . . from the grip of habit."

DESIREE: A Javanese dance.

MARIE: Maybe he's right.

DESIREE: Let him go. Listen to how beautiful it is.

MARIE: But I am letting him go.

DESIREE: Come.

[MARIE and DESIREE *dance again*.]

MARIE: Maybe he's right.

DESIREE: This time you can take bigger steps.

MARIE: Like this?

DESIREE: Excellent.

MARIE: Twenty-four hours ago, I wouldn't have believed it. How quickly a person can get over things.

DESIREE: You have no idea how quickly.

MARIE: Or do I only think so?

DESIREE [*brutally*]: You can't dance unless you concentrate. [*She turns off the gramophone.*]

MARIE [*quickly*]: But I am concentrating.

DESIREE: You were wrapped up in memories.

MARIE: I was only thinking about Alt, when he told me yesterday.

DESIREE: If Alt were more of a man—he would be a god.

MARIE: But he is a man.

DESIREE [*laughs*]: You have no instinct for this sort of thing. I could take a bath in his presence as if he were an old woman. Alt is sexless. [*She stretches out.*]

MARIE: What about his child?

DESIREE: He had a child out of love of children. That's even more incomprehensible in a man than it is in a woman. Alt is a male mama.

MARIE: Yesterday, he was very energetic.

DESIREE: He can be as implacable as a stupid, strict mama.

MARIE: He sticks his finger in your mouth to make you vomit.

DESIREE: If some day I can't go on . . .

MARIE [*near* DESIREE]: You?

DESIREE: I'd go to him.

MARIE: You, unable to go on?

DESIREE [*tenderly*]: You'll always stay with me?

MARIE [*strokes* DESIREE*'s hair*]: My little one.

DESIREE [*kisses* MARIE*'s hand*]: Marion.

MARIE [*removes her hand*]: No.

DESIREE: Put out the light. Let's dream.

[MARIE *is silent.*]

DESIREE: Come, we'll lie in my bed.

MARIE: No, I'm not tired yet. [*Pauses.*] Tomorrow is my bachelorette party.

DESIREE: How wonderfully childish.

MARIE: Whenever a person wants to do good, she always feels afterward it was childish. In fact, Freder was the one who played the role of the great debunker.

DESIREE: You can thank him.

MARIE: I don't want to see him.

DESIREE: It would do you good.

MARIE: No.

DESIREE: He and Alt are like two brothers who don't look alike.

MARIE [*astonished*]: Freder?

DESIREE: Both of them go all the way, without prejudice.

MARIE: Freder scares me somehow.

DESIREE: Somehow Alt scares me. It seems weird to me that he dresses like a man.

MARIE: Oh, you see everything in a sexual light.

DESIREE: They both have the same head, but on different bodies. They have different hands and may even have different hearts. But the same head. A human being is a funny composite. You don't know Freder when he loses his mind.

MARIE: He can lose his mind?

DESIREE: Otherwise, I wouldn't have put up with him so long. He sucks the blood beneath your skin like a beast of prey. It stops being orgasmic lust, it's delirium, pain, bestial madness. These are the rare instants in our life when we totally transcend the wretched creature within, and nothing's left of our body but a carcass.

MARIE [*quietly*]: I can't recognize your face.

DESIREE [*firmly embraces her*]: To die, Marion, to die.

MARIE: Die?

DESIREE: Just one little step beyond the fever of lust, one more little step beyond pain—and you never wake up again. [*Kisses her passionately.*] It would be magnificent, Marion.

MARIE [*sobs; pulls* DESIREE *to her*]: Don't die, don't die.

DESIREE: We'll die together, Marion.

[DESIREE *and* MARION *are seated, pressed against one another.*]

DESIREE: What's the point of going on? Sometimes you cheat to get away from things, then you wake up: and it's still the same mess. Still the same mess. What's the point? [*Pauses.*] I don't have the courage. If at such a moment I were to whisper in Freder's ear, "Sink your teeth into my throat! Murder me!"—he'd do it.

MARIE: Let yourself be murdered? Why not do it yourself, you know?

DESIREE: It's easier to let someone else murder you. It's more certain. But I don't have the courage. We are animals in a snare. In the snare of the desire to taste even that ultimate lustful pleasure while fully conscious. I have trained Freder for that—in case I make up my mind someday. But I don't have the courage. Two little words, when he's on the point of losing his mind. Two little words—"Murder me!"—and he'll do it. He'll sink his teeth into my throat. He knows how dangerous it is for him.

MARIE: Don't go on.

DESIREE: I've trained him like a wild beast, he only needs to be aroused.

MARIE [*delicately pulls free from* DESIREE]: No, little girl.

DESIREE: And he'll do it someday. Not to me, unfortunately. The spell is broken.

MARIE: Don't die.

DESIREE [*smiles*]: Now your eyes are bright blue.

MARIE: Don't talk.

DESIREE: How beautiful you are, Marion.

MARIE [*smiles*]: Sitting quietly, beside one another.

DESIREE: Staying together.

MARIE: Staying together. Don't talk. [*Pauses.*]

DESIREE [*smiles*]: You know—

MARIE: Yes?

DESIREE: Now I could even—

MARIE: Say it.

DESIREE [*laughs*]: Take up my crib notes.

MARIE: Anatomy.

DESIREE: The exam isn't for three weeks.

MARIE: It went well yesterday—

DESIREE: It's crazy, some people cram night and day, and flunk. I don't get it.

MARIE: I had to cram night and day.

DESIREE: Was it so hard?

MARIE: No, it was lovely.

DESIREE: If only one could find what comes easily lovely.

MARIE: To each his own oddity.

DESIREE [*takes candy from a box*]: Have some.

[DESIREE *and* MARIE *eat.*]

DESIREE: Should we dance or go to bed?

MARIE: It's still too early. It's nice here. We should have some tea. [*She rings.*]

DESIREE: I'm going to lie in bed, and you can sit next to me.

MARIE: Are you tired?

DESIREE: You shouldn't go to bed only when you're tired, but also when you're in a good mood. I love bed. I feel sheltered, at home.

MARIE: Go on, little girl.

DESIREE: Don't leave me alone much longer.

[DESIREE *goes into her room.*]

MARIE [*timidly glances at the letter*]: "To escape from oneself . . . like the prairie mustang from the locked corral."

SCENE 2

[LUCY *enters.*]

MARIE: Make us some tea, please. What's wrong with you?

LUCY [*smiles*]: Frau Schimmelbrot.

MARIE: So what?

LUCY: Frau Schimmelbrot isn't home.

MARIE: You're out of tea?

LUCY: No.

MARIE [*holds out the candy*]: Help yourself.

LUCY: Thanks. We're both from Passau.

MARIE: I didn't know.

LUCY: I accidentally saw it on your registration form.

MARIE: What were you doing with my registration form today?

LUCY: A long time ago.

MARIE [*observes her*]: It's nice that you're from Passau too.

LUCY: I didn't dare tell you. My father worked for yours. My father's a carpenter.

MARIE: Why are you so cheerful today?

LUCY: Your father is a builder?

MARIE: Yes.

LUCY: That's all right, then.

MARIE: Why are you so cheerful today?

LUCY: It's lovely weather.

MARIE: You're going out?

LUCY [*smiles*]: Maybe.

MARIE: Then I'll make the tea myself.

LUCY: I won't be going out right away. My fiancé also worked for your father.

MARIE: You have a fiancé?

LUCY: My fiancé is an upholsterer.

MARIE: Why did you leave Passau?

LUCY: There are six of us.

MARIE: Are you going to get married soon?

LUCY: When I go back. It's nice that you're from Passau too.

MARIE [*laughs*]: Why is it nice?

LUCY [*indicating* DESIREE's *door*]: I wouldn't like to be from the city that young lady's from.

MARIE: Ah.

LUCY: But Passau's nice. All my brothers and sisters are from Passau. They're all away now. [*She exits.*]

[MARIE *winds up the gramophone and sits beside it.*]

SCENE 3

[IRENE *enters.*]

IRENE: May I speak to you?

[MARIE *is silent.*]

IRENE: Just a word.

[MARIE *is silent.*]

IRENE: We don't have to sit down.

MARIE [*quickly*]: Excuse me.

[MARIE *and* IRENE *sit.*]

IRENE: Could you turn off the gramophone for a minute?

MARIE: It bothers you?

IRENE: Never mind. I don't want there to be any misunderstanding between us.

MARIE: You prefer precision.

IRENE: Herr Petrell hasn't been to see you?

MARIE: You're lying.

IRENE: Will you let me speak?

MARIE: Petrell would never come to see me. He's a coward.

IRENE: It depends whose influence he's under.

MARIE [*laughs*]: Ah.

IRENE: No one lives by his own impulses alone.

MARIE: Under your influence he's courageous now.

IRENE: You're annoyed.

MARIE: You're training him to be a hero.

IRENE: You really enjoy this music?

[MARIE *is silent.*]

IRENE: I can barely hear myself speak.

MARIE: How filled out a person can be in twenty-four hours.

IRENE: Meaning?

MARIE: Your face is filled out. Calmer, more filled out.

IRENE: I've probably put on weight in the meantime.

MARIE: The angularity of your face is suddenly gone. You are beautiful.

[MARIE *gets up and turns off the gramophone.*]

IRENE: Thank God.

MARIE: Make yourself comfortable.

IRENE: Let's settle things objectively.

MARIE: Objectively, then.

IRENE: Herr Petrell—

MARIE: Objectively.

IRENE: Herr Petrell—

MARIE: Call him Otto. Herr Petrell on your lips is a lie.

IRENE: You're wrong. Things with us haven't gone as far as all that.

MARIE: I got a letter from him this morning.

IRENE: I know.

MARIE [*looks at her*]: He shows you his letters? Maybe you composed it together?

IRENE: He has his own style.

MARIE: I know. The prairie mustang in the corral.

IRENE: He's a poet.

MARIE: He is a poet.

IRENE: I've come to suggest that we be friends.

MARIE: Thank you.

IRENE: You've done a good deal for him.

MARIE: Thank you.

IRENE: You've helped him get through hard times.

MARIE [*irritated*]: Thank you.

IRENE: He will never forget it. He says nice things about you. You've been more than a mother to him.

MARIE [*beside herself*]: Will you shut up at last?

IRENE: I don't understand.

MARIE: You don't understand.

IRENE: You are too precious in his eyes to be erased from his life.

MARIE: The eyes of the prairie mustang.

IRENE: Figures of speech.

MARIE: Which might be your own. Do you write his articles for him too?

IRENE: A person can't talk to you.

MARIE: I'm not a fish.

IRENE: No one said you were.

[IRENE *stands up.*]

MARIE: Sit down.

IRENE: Marie.

MARIE: I am not a fish.

IRENE: What do you mean, you're not a fish?

MARIE: Come on, spit it out. What do you want?

IRENE: I wanted to offer you friendship.

MARIE: Thank you.

IRENE: That's the whole point of my mission.

MARIE: Thank you.

IRENE: Until such time as you come to your senses . . .

MARIE: Sit down.

IRENE: I don't want to spoil your musical evening.

MARIE: Sit down.

IRENE: I have things to do.

MARIE: Sit down.

IRENE: Don't play schoolma'rm.

MARIE: Sit down.

IRENE: You seem to be—

MARIE [*beside herself*]: Sit down.

IRENE [*sits*]: What's the meaning of this?

MARIE [*snatches the hat off* IRENE's *head*]: We have to take tea together.

IRENE: I have things to do.

MARIE: Right now you're in my home.

IRENE [*hesitant*]: I won't let you intimidate me.

MARIE: Thank you for your visit.

IRENE: I won't let you impose on me.

MARIE [*holds out the candy box*]: Help yourself.

IRENE: I don't care for sweets.

MARIE: A gift from Desiree. She gave me this box today. Kind of her, isn't it? The flowers are also from Desiree. Look around.

IRENE: It's a lovely gesture.

MARIE: No. It's a lovely box.

IRENE: What does that mean?

MARIE: Why—your friendship.

IRENE: Think it over calmly.

MARIE: What exactly is your friendship?

IRENE: Think it over calmly. You have plenty of time.

MARIE: I'm perfectly calm. Was this his idea?

IRENE: That's of no importance.

MARIE: In the letter he doesn't mention it.

IRENE: It occurred to us afterward.

MARIE: To whom?

IRENE: Obviously there was no need to put it in writing.

MARIE: I don't think it's so obvious.

IRENE: After two years living with you?

MARIE: That too—you taught him that.

IRENE: You seem to take him for a moron.

MARIE: For inconsiderate, indifferent. But his lack of consideration comes from his indifference. He's not a bad person.

IRENE: No one said he is.

MARIE: Even so, it never would have occurred to him to offer me his friendship today. It's an idea of yours.

IRENE: No matter.

MARIE: Yes, it is a great matter. Because you—you are a bad person.

IRENE: If that makes you feel better.

MARIE: You're doing it out of a sense of order.

[IRENE *laughs*.]

MARIE: You also calculate the right amount of emotion.

IRENE: I had no idea.

MARIE: You taught him just how much gratitude poses no danger to you.

IRENE: Go on talking. It seems to do you good.

MARIE: Everything about you is calculated, nothing comes from feelings. You are a fish.

IRENE: So now I'm the fish.

MARIE: You keep your objective in your line of sight.

IRENE: I don't deny it.

MARIE: Your ambition works like a machine, with no consideration or scruples, right to the goal.

IRENE: It's cost me enough to achieve that.

MARIE: I know.

IRENE: I didn't do my studying lying in bed.

MARIE: I know.

IRENE: But in an unheated room.

MARIE: To reach your goal, you would have gone hungry.

IRENE: I did go hungry.

MARIE: Because you're proud of it.

IRENE: Of going hungry?

MARIE: Of going hungry.

IRENE: You leap to surprising conclusions.

MARIE: You tell everyone that you went hungry to carry on your studies.

IRENE: Because a young woman who's not too plain can earn money by other means.

MARIE: No one would accuse you of that.

IRENE: There's no need to accuse young people. They're capable of anything. It's not enough to survive the battle of being young. You have to win it—that is the secret of people with a purpose.

MARIE [*quietly*]: I don't want to win.

IRENE: A younger generation that is wide awake but unsure of its place teeters on the brink of imminent peril to its life. It's mere chance that it isn't destroyed.

MARIE: I don't want to win.

IRENE: You'll get over it.

[MARIE *stares at her.*]

IRENE: We survive whatever we want to survive.

MARIE: You know that in advance, do you?

[IRENE *is silent.*]

MARIE: Is that why you came?

IRENE: We'll end up being friends.

MARIE: Do you need me?

[IRENE *looks at her, unsure.*]

MARIE: Are you going to stand by me?

IRENE: If you like.

MARIE: I don't.

IRENE: Then excuse my persistence.

[IRENE *rises.*]

MARIE: I never want to see you again, you or him.

IRENE: We're in agreement there.

MARIE: I hate your whole phony act.

IRENE: Don't get upset.

MARIE: Your goodness, your kind intentions—the whole phony act! Making a game of your power. You won't beat me down.

IRENE: Let's part calmly.

MARIE: I see right through you—you Irma, you.

IRENE: Now you're just being rude.

MARIE: Didn't you tell me yourself?

IRENE: And what if my name is Irma?

MARIE: But you call yourself Irene. Everything about you is phony.

[IRENE *heads for the door.*]

MARIE: How could a doorman's daughter call herself Irene?

IRENE: Let me go.

MARIE [*barring her way*]: Sit.

IRENE: You've lost your mind.

MARIE: Sit down.

IRENE: Let me go. [*Touches* MARIE.]

MARIE [*pushes* IRENE *away*]: Sit down, Irma.

IRENE: I'll call for help.

MARIE: Call, Irma. He won't hear you downstairs.

IRENE [*advancing on* MARIE]: I won't let you stand in my way.

MARIE [*grabbing* IRENE *violently by the hair*]: This is the prairie, isn't it? The red prairie? Why did you let your hair grow long?

IRENE [*beside herself*]: Let me alone, you—

MARIE [*laughs*]: To be different. It's all phony.

IRENE: I'll slap your face.

[IRENE *and* MARIE *struggle*.]

MARIE [*laughing*]: He's waiting for you downstairs. Don't worry. He's someone who can be trained for anything. You've figured him out perfectly, my little Irma. [*She drags* IRENE *through the room and ties her by her hair to the foot of the dresser*.] Thalassa! Thalassa! Freder's war cry. Now we'll play Redskins on the Prairie. [*Laughs hysterically*.] Redhead. Redhead. Tied to a dresser. To a prairie dresser. [*Leaps up*.] Now let's go get the prairie mustang.

[MARIE *exits*.]

IRENE [*shouting after* MARIE, *beside herself*]: You'll kill yourself. [*She tries to untie her hair*.]

SCENE 4

[FREDER *comes out of* DESIREE's *room.*]

FREDER: Why are you sitting on the floor?

IRENE: She'll pay for this.

FREDER: You seem to be tied by your hair.

IRENE: She'll pay for this.

FREDER: Not easy to untie.

IRENE: You're hurting me.

FREDER: You have thick hair.

IRENE: Let go, I'd rather do it myself.

FREDER: Beautiful thick hair. What did you come here for?

IRENE: We were feeling sorry for her.

FREDER: If you rush, you're going to get your hair even more tangled. [*He helps her again.*]

IRENE: As things are now, she's liable to kill him.

FREDER: He's waiting for you downstairs?

IRENE: No, he isn't.

FREDER: But nearby?

IRENE: Take your hands off.

FREDER [*laughs*]: Only if I want to. This is how people get into predicaments, Girlsie, and all of a sudden it's too late. I can do with you what I want, you little witch. Are you ticklish?

IRENE [*furious*]: Let go of me.

FREDER: You've never slept with a man, have you?

IRENE: I'm dying with desire to make you my confession.

FREDER: First the altar, only then the bed. You're pulling out whole tufts.

IRENE [*free, rapidly putting herself to rights in the mirror*]: You will never see me here again.

[IRENE *exits.*]

FREDER: Won't he be surprised to see such a mess.

[FREDER *goes into* DESIREE'*s room.*]

SCENE 5

[LUCY *enters with a tea tray.*]

LUCY [*at* DESIREE'*s door*]: Would you like me to bring in the tea?

[FREDER *appears.*]

FREDER: Who's it for?

LUCY [*quietly*]: Fräulein Marie ordered it.

FREDER: Put it on the table.

[LUCY *places the tray on the table.*]

FREDER: Is that your Sunday dress?

LUCY: Yes.

FREDER: Come here. Look at me.

LUCY: Herr Freder.

FREDER: Why are you smiling? Are you happy?

LUCY: Frau Schimmelbrot isn't home.

FREDER: Where is Frau Schimmelbrot?

LUCY: I don't know.

FREDER: Did Frau Schimmelbrot go to a dance?

LUCY: I don't know.

FREDER: Does she go out often?

LUCY: No, rarely.

FREDER: Then she's definitely gone to a dance. She didn't look for her rings?

LUCY: She hasn't noticed a thing.

FREDER: Then she hasn't gone to a dance, but to her poor relations. Why are you laughing? You don't show off jewels to poor relations.

LUCY [*laughs*]: No.

FREDER: Would you like to go?

LUCY: Whenever you'd like.

FREDER: There's plenty of time. [*He pours the tea.*] Sit down.

[LUCY *laughs.*]

FREDER: Why are you laughing?

LUCY: I'm so happy.

FREDER: Drink. [*He holds out the candy box.*]

LUCY: Fräulein Marie already offered me some.

FREDER: Eat and drink.

[FREDER *abruptly goes back into* DESIREE's *room. The door remains open.*]

FREDER [*offstage*]: If I may.

[DESIREE *laughs offstage.*]

FREDER [*offstage*]: For Fräulein Lucy.

DESIREE [*offstage*]: What a gag! [*She laughs.*]

FREDER [*offstage*]: Stay in bed. I'll find it on my own.

[LUCY *listens nervously.*]

DESIREE [*offstage*]: You're going out with her?

FREDER: Yes.

[FREDER *reenters with a powder puff and sticks of makeup.*]

FREDER: Stay seated, Lucy.

LUCY [*frightened*]: Herr Freder.

FREDER: Tomorrow I'll buy some just for you.

[FREDER *sits, facing* LUCY.]

FREDER: Head higher.

LUCY [*quietly*]: I don't know how to do it.

FREDER: I'll show you. Especially the eyes. [*He starts to make* LUCY *up.*]

LUCY: Herr Freder.

FREDER: Why are you so nervous?

LUCY: Does it suit me?

FREDER: You've got to leave it to me.

LUCY: Yes.

FREDER: Don't move your head. You've never held a powder puff?

LUCY: No.

FREDER: Natural beauty is only a base.

LUCY [*naively*]: Yes.

FREDER: Nature is there so you can adjust it to your wishes. A woman awakes only through her makeup.

LUCY: Yes.

FREDER: You have an animated face. But it will be attractive only when you give it a precise expression. I'm almost done. Why are you trembling? Does it itch?

LUCY: Herr Freder.

FREDER [*laughs*]: Exciting, isn't it? You'd like to throw yourself around my neck, right?

[LUCY *is silent.*]

FREDER: The cheeks now.

LUCY: I know.

FREDER: What do you know?

LUCY: You think I'm ugly.

FREDER: Ridiculous.

LUCY: You wouldn't make me up otherwise.

FREDER: You're beautiful. But it has to be brought out.

LUCY [*still doubtful*]: Yes.

FREDER: Natural beauty smells of carbolic soap. Don't move your lips.

LUCY [*quickly*]: Herr Freder.

FREDER: Now what?

LUCY: You won't want to kiss me anymore.

FREDER [*laughs*]: You're crazy.

LUCY: The red color on my lips must make you puke.

FREDER: Hold still.

LUCY: No, Herr Freder, please.

FREDER [*making her up by force*]: Stupid kid.

LUCY: Please, not the lips.

FREDER: You'll see how I'll kiss you afterward.

LUCY [*unresisting*]: Herr Freder.

FREDER: Now look in the mirror.

[LUCY *stands, takes a long look in the mirror.*]

LUCY: That's not me.

FREDER: It is you, living up to your potential. You see how beautiful you are?

[LUCY *is silent.*]

FREDER: I'll go and get you a lovely evening wrap.

LUCY: Please, Herr Freder, please don't.

FREDER: And a little hat.

LUCY [*dizzy*]: No.

FREDER: Then we'll walk out together.

[FREDER *goes into* DESIREE'*s room.*]

[LUCY *sinks onto a chair.*]

[FREDER *reenters with* DESIREE'*s wrap and hat.*]

FREDER: Why are you crying? Hold your head high. Your mascara will run. Here, take my handkerchief.

[LUCY *dries her eyes.*]

FREDER [*helping her put on the wrap*]: You're laughing now, eh?

[LUCY *stares at him.*]

FREDER: Laugh.

[LUCY *smiles.*]

FREDER: Really laugh. [*He kisses* LUCY *on the mouth.*]

LUCY [*comforted*]: Herr Freder.

FREDER: A little mouth made of honey. Are you happy?

LUCY [*with a warm smile*]: If you like me better this way.

FREDER: Now you are beautiful.

LUCY: Plus the hat. [*She puts it on.*]

FREDER: All at once, it's perfect.

[LUCY *looks in the mirror.*]

FREDER: You'll make conquests.

LUCY: I'm ashamed.

FREDER: People will turn their heads when you go by.

LUCY: I feel so funny.

FREDER: People will accost you.

LUCY: Nobody would dare if you're with me.

FREDER: And what if I'm not?

LUCY: You're going to leave me alone?

FREDER: Would you enjoy that?

LUCY: I'd drown myself.

FREDER: And if I don't want you to drown yourself?

LUCY: Then I won't.

FREDER: Because you love me.

LUCY: I love you a lot.

FREDER: And what if I insist that you be accosted?

LUCY [*worried*]: I don't understand what you mean.

FREDER: A good-looking young man, one you'd like.

LUCY: No, Herr Freder.

FREDER: Look in the mirror. A rich young man might find you attractive.

LUCY: What do I care?

FREDER: You love me alone, eh? Come on.

LUCY: Are we going to a fancy dress ball? I've never been to a fancy dress ball.

FREDER: You think you're in fancy dress?

LUCY [*laughs*]: Especially my face.

[DESIREE *appears in the doorway.*]

DESIREE: Let me look at you, Fräulein Lucy.

LUCY [*frightened*]: For heaven's sake.

[LUCY *exits.*]

DESIREE: That's a pretty get-up!

FREDER [*laughs*]: She's embarrassed.

DESIREE: You want her to go on the streets?

FREDER: Thank you ever so much.

[FREDER *exits*.]

SCENE 6

[MARIE *and* PETRELL *enter*.]

MARIE: Come in. [*To* DESIREE.] Leave us alone.

[DESIREE *goes into her room*.]

[MARIE *pulls* PETRELL *into the room*.]

MARIE: She isn't here now. She who waited so patiently for you. It took too long for her. [*Laughs*.]

PETRELL: Where is Irene?

MARIE: It took too long for her. Why were you hiding so far away? Have a seat.

[PETRELL *remains standing*.]

PETRELL: What do you want?

MARIE: Not you. Don't worry.

PETRELL: What do you want?

MARIE: I'd rather run down the streets like a stupid cow wondering who owns her. Have a seat.

PETRELL: When you're calmer.

MARIE: I'm very calm.

PETRELL: I know you too well.

MARIE: Thank you.

PETRELL: You really want us to part this way?

MARIE: Keep your honeyed tones for others.

PETRELL: Let me explain.

MARIE: If I chose to act, you'd never go back to her again. Anybody could wrap you around her little finger.

PETRELL: It's impossible to talk to you.

MARIE: Why is it impossible to talk to me?

PETRELL: But you don't talk.

MARIE: Do I sing?

PETRELL: You gasp.

MARIE [*laughs*]: I gasp.

PETRELL: So to speak.

MARIE: And she's got a flute in her mouth.

PETRELL: Stop it at last.

MARIE While I gasp.

PETRELL: I didn't say you gasp.

MARIE: You did say I gasp.

PETRELL: I meant that you're overexcited.

MARIE: You said that I gasp.

PETRELL: If you insist.

MARIE: Who told you that I want anything?

PETRELL: Then why drag me here?

MARIE: So you could pick up Irene.

PETRELL: You're lying.

MARIE: So you could take her away with you.

PETRELL: She's been gone a long time, and you ran after her.

MARIE [*laughs*]: She hadn't gone.

PETRELL: She would have prevented you from dropping down on me like that.

MARIE [*laughs*]: Prevention is sometimes not so easy.

PETRELL: You ran after her and overtook her.

MARIE: You're no good at reconstructing. Look, maybe you'll find a piece of her in the room.

PETRELL: I'd better visit you another day.

MARIE: A piece of her prairie in the room.

PETRELL: When you're calmer.

MARIE: Sniff her out, mustang, sniff her out.

PETRELL: I'd had enough.

[PETRELL *tries to leave.*]

MARIE: Look, mustang, prairies, red prairies. Cold. Cold. [*Laughs.*] If you go to the dresser, you'll get warm, very warm.

[MARIE *pushes* PETRELL *to the dresser.*]

MARIE: Open your eyes. You still see nothing? [*Triumphant.*] There it is—the red prairie.

[MARIE *shoves a few hanks of* IRENE's *hair in* PETRELL's *face.*]

PETRELL [*frightened*]: What have you done?

MARIE: We were playing Red Indians.

PETRELL [*horrified*]: Marie.

MARIE [*with a huge laugh*]: Red Indians. As you wrote in your letter, mustang. I scalped her. Scalped Big Chief Red Skull.

PETRELL [*horrified, grabbing her*]: Marie.

[MARIE *suddenly falls silent. She stares at* PETRELL.]

PETRELL [*quietly*]: What have you done with her?

[MARIE *stares at him with wide-open eyes.*]

PETRELL: Did you—?

MARIE [*quietly*]: Let go of me.

PETRELL: Have you gone crazy?

MARIE: Don't ever touch me again.

PETRELL: I want to know what you've done with her.

MARIE: Nothing.

PETRELL [*forcefully*]: Where is Irene?

MARIE [*suddenly*]: And what if I murdered her?

PETRELL: I don't believe it now.

MARIE: I murdered her.

PETRELL: I don't believe it.

MARIE: A minute ago you were afraid I had.

PETRELL: But now I don't believe it.

MARIE: You were afraid I had.

PETRELL: I don't believe you're capable of it.

MARIE: You may be mistaken.

PETRELL: I see it in your eyes.

MARIE: Such a keen observer of human behavior.

PETRELL: So where is she?

MARIE: Lying on the kitchen floor. The police are on their way. The coroner is in the kitchen too.

PETRELL: You've hidden her.

MARIE: Ask the coroner. I throttled her. If you stay, they'll arrest you too.

PETRELL: You've locked her in. In Desiree's room?

MARIE: If I were you, I wouldn't ask so many questions. I'll go to the kitchen. Are you afraid to?

PETRELL: You enjoy seeing me suffer.

MARIE [*changing course*]: Nothing happened to her.

PETRELL: Then where is she?

MARIE: At home.

PETRELL: At home?

MARIE: Or at your place. Do you love her a lot?

PETRELL: You went downstairs with her?

MARIE [*worn out*]: I tied her here so that she couldn't hold me back. She will be very useful to you. You will go far. She is very clever.

PETRELL [*aghast*]: By her hair?

MARIE [*nods*]: Tell me about the time you first fell in love with her.

PETRELL: How brutal.

MARIE: I am so sorry. Do you love her a lot?

PETRELL: Leave me alone now.

MARIE: Does it hurt you? Can't you forgive me?

PETRELL: I'm leaving.

MARIE: Can't you forgive me? Kiss me.

PETRELL: I have to go now.

MARIE: Hatred. Hatred eternal? With her help you will have a career.

PETRELL: I told her at the time that it was a mistake.

MARIE: What was a mistake?

PETRELL: Good-bye.

MARIE: Coming here? It was a mistake. You know me better than she does. You wouldn't let yourself be persuaded. Say something—answer me.

PETRELL: Still, I would never have thought you capable of such brutality.

MARIE: She'll have a career too. You'll both have careers.

[PETRELL *is about to leave.*]

MARIE [*suddenly*]: Hit me—go on.

PETRELL: You're not in your right mind.

MARIE: Hit me, since you can't forgive me.

PETRELL: You want the whole house to hear it?

MARIE: Since you despise me.

PETRELL: Words will get us nowhere.

MARIE: Hit me—go on.

PETRELL: Don't shout.

MARIE: What do I have to do to make you hit me? I hit her, all right. I tied her up by her hair. I tied her up like a mangy bitch. [*Beside herself.*] Go on—hit me.

[PETRELL *tries to reach the door.*]

MARIE: Stay. You don't skip out like that when you've loved a woman for two years. Or was it all a swindle?

PETRELL: I can't stand this.

[PETRELL *opens the door.*]

MARIE [*beside herself*]: What about my money?

PETRELL: Your money?

MARIE: My money. Or wasn't I supporting you?

[PETRELL *quickly closes the door.*]

PETRELL: Do you want the whole house to hear you?

MARIE: Let the whole house hear me. You let me feed you for two years.

PETRELL [*livid*]: Are you insane?

MARIE: That got him where he lives. Who let me buy him everything? For whose sake did I give private lessons late into the night so I could buy him groceries? For whom did I buy suits and books and shoes and shirts and socks?

PETRELL: I shall return the money.

MARIE: You'll leave me high and dry. She'll keep her money to herself.

PETRELL: I earn a living.

MARIE: Who got blisters on her feet looking for a job for you?

PETRELL: I don't deny it.

MARIE: Who sent you to a health spa because of a lung disease that was pure fiction?

PETRELL: This is getting embarrassing.

MARIE: And now he's getting embarrassed.

PETRELL: This is how they interrogate a thief.

MARIE: Aren't you a thief?

PETRELL: Marie.

MARIE: Are you or aren't you a thief?

PETRELL: You don't know what you're saying.

MARIE: You are a thief.

PETRELL: I've had enough of this.

[PETRELL *heads for the door.*]

MARIE: Go on, hit me if you're not a thief.

PETRELL: The whole house can listen in, for all I care.

MARIE: Hit me—go on.

[MARIE *holds* PETRELL *tight.*]

MARIE: Go on, hit me if you're not a thief. Can't you take pity on me?

PETRELL: Someone should pour a bucket of ice water over you.

[MARIE *falls to her knees.*]

MARIE [*sobbing*]: Go on, hit me if you're not a thief.

PETRELL: This madness is getting contagious.

[PETRELL *pulls loose.*]

MARIE: I won't let you go until you hit me. I won't let go of you.

PETRELL: You belong in a madhouse.

[PETRELL *exits.*]

MARIE: Hit me. Hit me. Hit me.

SCENE 7

[DESIREE *comes out of her room, kneels beside* MARIE.]

DESIREE: Marion.

MARIE [*smiling*]: Hit me. You're not a thief.

[DESIREE *helps* MARIE *rise.*]

DESIREE: Poor little girl.

MARIE: He didn't hit me.

DESIREE: Come. I'll kiss your tears away.

MARIE: Yes. Kiss me.

DESIREE: My little Marion.

MARIE: He didn't hit me. Kiss me again.

DESIREE [*kissing her passionately*]: We'll lie down in my bed, pressed tight together, and we'll be warm again.

MARIE: Pressed tight together.

DESIREE: Warm again, as when I was a child. I'll tell you lots of stories. Marion. Like two little sisters before they fall asleep.

MARIE: Like two little sisters before they fall asleep, when the light is put out. You are my sister.

DESIREE: You are mine.

[DESIREE *and* MARIE *embrace.*]

[*Curtain.*]

ACT III

[*Evening.*]

SCENE 1

[MARIE, DESIREE, FREDER, ALT *enter.*]

FREDER [*stretched out*]: I can feel my liver.

ALT: Don't drink so much.

FREDER: My liver is going to my head.

DESIREE: You'll end up collapsing.

FREDER: I always sleep with my knees up to my chin.

DESIREE [*laughs*]: For heaven's sake.

FREDER: It doesn't hurt as much.

DESIREE: It's about time you got married.

FREDER: I ask for your hand, Marie.

MARIE [*laughing*]: Idiot.

DESIREE: He's asking for your hand in earnest.

FREDER: Totally in earnest. We would make a perfect couple.

DESIREE: She'll think about it. These last few days, she's learned to appreciate you.

FREDER: I'm going to reform.

DESIREE: He's going to reform.

FREDER: Drink more water.

DESIREE: Why don't you answer him?

FREDER [*rises*]: When the time comes, with eyes wide open, one should join the middle class.

DESIREE: Bravo. His intentions are honorable.

[MARIE *stares at her.*]

DESIREE: His liver has led him to reason. I'm not joking.

FREDER [*writhing*]: I'm in pain.

DESIREE: Don't stare at me like that, Marion.

ALT: What does pain matter?

[ALT *stretches out.*]

FREDER [*to* MARIE]: Think it over.

MARIE: Leave me alone.

FREDER: I want someone to see to my needs. I don't like to work. You, on the contrary, love to work. So we're complementary. I've been calling you by your first name for three days now, so marriage is nothing but a matter of form.

DESIREE: Freder is a stickler for form.

FREDER: I promise willingly, the moment you say yes, to break off all relations with Lucy.

DESIREE: You still have relations with her?

FREDER: She surpasses all my expectations.

MARIE: Well, then, marry Lucy.

FREDER: I'm not a pimp.

DESIREE: You don't understand him.

MARIE: Do you think this is funny?

DESIREE: Either you join the middle class or you commit suicide. There's no other way out. I'm not joking.

FREDER [*to* MARIE]: And besides, we kissed.

MARIE [*laughs*]: You were dropped on your heads, the two of you.

FREDER: You deny it?

DESIREE: When did you kiss?

FREDER: Last night.

MARIE: You were there.

DESIREE: I don't remember.

MARIE: You urged us to do it.

DESIREE: You're dreaming.

MARIE: You wouldn't give us a moment's peace, Daisy. At last I had to kiss him.

DESIREE: I missed it completely.

MARIE: When you're drunk you miss a lot of things.

FREDER: Every time I breathe it cuts me like a knife. God damn.

DESIREE: Not so loud. Alt is sleeping.

ALT: Pain is not an organic modification of cellular tissue. Even with a bullet in his body, a soldier can keep running as if nothing had happened.

DESIREE: When somebody steps on my little toe, I reach for my revolver.

ALT: But when tubercle bacilli are devouring your lungs, you don't feel a thing. Pain is an end in itself.

MARIE: I've often stepped on your feet.

DESIREE: I've stopped dancing with you.

MARIE [*laughs*]: She's fed up with me.

DESIREE: Don't leave Freder without an answer.

ALT: A stimulus, a psychic process, an autosuggestion subtly interrupted whenever we cry in pain.

FREDER: I need to take a hot footbath.

[FREDER *exits.*]

MARIE [*quietly, to* DESIREE]: You're fed up with me?

[DESIREE *is silent.*]

MARIE: Go on, say it.

ALT: Our nervous system runs between these two poles, sleep and pain. We love them both. Both of them, just like total nonexistence, provide the greatest satisfaction of our existence.

DESIREE: I've finally discovered a brilliant trick to bring them together, those two poles.

[ALT *stares at* DESIREE.]

DESIREE: Pain and sleep at the same time. Go on talking, Alt. More tea, please.

[MARIE *pours tea for* DESIREE.]

DESIREE [*to* MARIE]: More sugar and cognac in it. [*To* ALT.] Don't wear out your brains.

ALT: I'm not wearing out my brains.

DESIREE: You've guessed it?

MARIE: What is he supposed to guess?

DESIREE: Be quiet, baby. Think of your poet instead.

MARIE: Him.

DESIREE: If you don't intervene, they'll get married.

MARIE: I'll put the orange blossoms on their heads myself.

DESIREE: He'll be faithful till death do them part. With her masculine authority she'll dominate him even when she's a grandmother. Better be quick, Marion.

MARIE: You're jilting me?

DESIREE: You cling, it's in your nature. All I want is to see you settled.

MARIE: I can manage, even without you.

DESIREE: Freder's marriage proposal is still on the table.

[MARIE *embraces* DESIREE.]

MARIE: For the last few days all she does is quarrel with me.

DESIREE [*pulling loose*]: Let go of me.

MARIE: But it will soon pass.

DESIREE: She stages these marital scenes. Some women can live only on terms of marriage, even with a woman.

MARIE: You're being mean today.

DESIREE: Now I understand why Boysie doesn't put up with you.

MARIE [*quietly*]: You.

DESIREE: After a while, it becomes insufferable. You've got to kick that habit.

MARIE: Won't you give me a kiss?

DESIREE: No, I won't. Sit still.

[MARIE *sits*.]

DESIREE: She reminds me of that industrialist from Hamburg who was eager to marry me. A very pretty fellow. He fainted away once when I casually kissed him. Even when he spent the night with a prostitute, he lived that night with her as husband and wife. He told her about his mother, his business, and his views on improving the political situation in Germany.

MARIE: I'm going to have a gray *mouliné* cloak made, wraparound style.

DESIREE: Tomorrow you have a fitting for the two-piece.

MARIE: Tomorrow afternoon.

DESIREE: I'll go with you. The jacket shouldn't be cut too low in front.

MARIE: You can show him.

ALT: Where did you get your pajamas? You are both ravishing.

DESIREE: Marion especially. [*To* MARIE, *tenderly*.] In blue, I could eat you up. That blue, I was the one who picked it out. It goes so well with your hair.

[DESIREE *kisses* MARIE.]

MARIE: Now we're on good terms again.

DESIREE: She always has to make a statement.

MARIE: I won't do it anymore.

DESIREE: It's horrible.

MARIE: What's horrible?

DESIREE: To be registered. To come to conclusions. The daily routine. Married life. It's stifling.

ALT: Out with it. What's come over you?

DESIREE: Spare me.

ALT: I'm going to put my finger down your throat.

DESIREE: No thanks.

ALT: Everyone needs a chance to unburden himself. To go to the toilet, psychologically.

DESIREE: And now it's my turn.

ALT [*firmly*]: We won't desert you.

DESIREE: What do I care about moral principles?

ALT: It's not a moral principle. It is the only social responsibility to others.

DESIREE: You're getting sentimental.

ALT: You have the right to do whatever you please with yourself. But the primary condition of existence, the only negation of existential madness, is that each person live his life to the end. Kill someone else instead. Anyone who kills himself becomes a mortal danger to all the others.

DESIREE: That's the first time I've heard empty phrases out of your mouth.

MARIE: It's not a phrase. It's the only divine feeling we have within us.

ALT: Bravo! Have some cocaine.

DESIREE: This time we don't see eye to eye. Freder understands me better.

ALT: Freder will never lay hands on himself.

DESIREE: He likes it here. But as for other people, he won't stop them.

ALT: Even the criminal feels socially responsible for the group.

DESIREE: No cocaine. Veronal, a lovely big dose of Veronal. You glide gently into sleep, you get lost in its depths—and at last it's all over.

MARIE: Am I such a stranger to you?

DESIREE: Little Marion.

MARIE: That kind of thought comes over you only when you've stopped caring about anyone.

DESIREE [*tenderly*]: Don't be sad, Marion.

MARIE [*smiling*]: I only make statements.

DESIREE: We probably spend all our lives as strangers.

MARIE: You're not a stranger to me.

DESIREE: We're of different natures. At heart, no one is a stranger to you, but to me everyone is. We've tried it out, little one.

ALT: You haven't tried long enough.

DESIREE [*smiles*]: How long do you have to try? She doesn't fit. I didn't need to sleep with her every night to find that out.

MARIE [*quietly*]: You disenchant everything.

DESIREE: Perhaps. All enchantments contain the germs of disgust. You don't fit, Marion.

MARIE [*nods*]: I'm not made for it.

DESIREE: She does whatever I tell her to. But she misses the mark.

MARIE: I don't fit.

DESIREE: The first night I brought you from the floor to my bed, I really felt I was possessing you. But it wasn't me, it was pain that made you relax.

MARIE: Be quiet.

DESIREE: She's ashamed in front of you. Alt isn't a man. Alt is a misbegotten woman—you could strip naked, calm as you please, in his presence. The very next night I thought the two of us rather comical.

MARIE: Be quiet at last.

DESIREE: I've been very patient with you. I wouldn't have been as patient with a man.

MARIE: I don't have an Adam's apple.

DESIREE [*laughs*]: You're my little fool.

MARIE: When I was a little girl I played with dolls, not with wooden horses and swords.

[DESIREE *embraces* MARIE*'s knees.*]

DESIREE [*to* MARIE]: My little innocent love.

MARIE [*quietly*]: I need the illusion of a man.

DESIREE: Are you unhappy?

MARIE [*quietly*]: Yes.

DESIREE: I've disappointed her too.

MARIE: Yes.

[DESIREE *kisses* MARIE.]

DESIREE [*to* MARIE]: Poor wretches that we are.

[DESIREE *and* MARIE *embrace; a pause.*]

DESIREE: Where are we heading? Two years from now, I'll have my degree, as you do today. Is that the ideal? What do you dream of?

MARIE: I've stopped dreaming.

DESIREE: Medical orderly at the general hospital. Odors of iodine and carbolic. That stench all one's life long.

MARIE: It used to be music to me.

DESIREE: The most repulsive treatments, all life long, on unwashed strangers.

MARIE: It used to be music to me to relieve the pain of thousands of people.

DESIREE: I've never believed in other people. How gauche, to lose oneself for the sake of others. Even when you relieve their pain, they prefer to be alone.

SCENE 2

[LUCY *enters, showily dressed.*]

LUCY [*slightly tipsy*]: Do the ladies and gents need anything else?

DESIREE: Why are you dressed like that?

LUCY: Do the ladies and gents need anything else?

MARIE: You're going out?

LUCY [*nods*]: I have to.

DESIREE: Alone?

LUCY [*smiles*]: They don't leave me alone for long.

DESIREE: Who don't leave you alone for long?

LUCY: I don't care who.

DESIREE: Come and sit with us.

LUCY: I'll be late.

DESIREE: We're depressed. Cheer us up a bit.

LUCY: I'm never sad.

DESIREE: You're such a cheerful creature.

LUCY: Lovely, lovely, life is lovely.

DESIREE: What a pretty voice you have.

LUCY [*suddenly*]: I'll be right back.

[LUCY *exits*.]

DESIREE: Poor creature, and yet I envy her.

MARIE: How does he manage it?

DESIREE: Freder?

MARIE [*nods*]: To lose the need to think for oneself. To submit to someone else's will, so that you think you're looked after and don't have to care for yourself.

DESIREE: You'll never go on the streets.

MARIE: But to be free from oneself at last?

DESIREE: I could imitate her, without numbing my willpower, without Freder, voluntarily.

SCENE 3

[LUCY *enters with wine and glasses*.]

DESIREE: We already have cognac.

LUCY: This is good wine.

ALT: Where did you get this wine?

LUCY: I can bring another bottle.

DESIREE: I could kiss you.

LUCY: I'd like to have a drink with you.

MARIE [*laughs*]: We Passau girls.

LUCY [*laughs*]: I'd completely forgotten about Passau.

MARIE: What about your fiancé?

LUCY: My fiancé.

DESIREE: She has a fiancé?

MARIE: In Passau.

DESIREE: She has a fiancé in Passau.

LUCY: Go on, laugh, Fräulein.

DESIREE: You can call me Desiree.

LUCY [*laughs*]: I don't hate you anymore.

DESIREE [*astonished*]: You hated me?

LUCY: A lot.

DESIREE: Why?

[LUCY *is silent.*]

MARIE: I feel so miserable.

ALT: Come and lie down beside me.

DESIREE: And now you don't?

LUCY: Don't be mad. You're so beautiful, Fräulein.

DESIREE: Call me Desiree.

LUCY: I don't understand Herr Freder.

DESIREE: What don't you understand?

LUCY: Why he doesn't love you anymore.

DESIREE: But you're happy.

LUCY: I'm lucky.

DESIREE: You love him very much.

LUCY: You can't love a man more.

DESIREE: That's beautiful. Kiss me.

[DESIREE *and* LUCY *embrace.*]

ALT: Despite everything she's been through, she's still a child.

LUCY: All we need is music. We'll sit and listen.

DESIREE [*winding up the gramophone*]: Let's dance.

LUCY: The doctor doesn't dance.

DESIREE: When is Freder coming for you?

LUCY: I go out by myself. He trusts me.

DESIREE: He takes your money?

LUCY: Not a penny. Yet I owe him everything.

DESIREE: You make a lot? Tell me.

LUCY: It depends.

DESIREE: Tell me.

LUCY: I even got a marriage proposal.

DESIREE: You can't consider it.

LUCY: He shouldn't hold his breath.

DESIREE: You could set up a little apartment.

LUCY [*quickly*]: No.

DESIREE: Frau Schimmelbrot will get on to you.

LUCY: I'm not worried.

DESIREE: I've got it now. Because Freder lives here.

LUCY [*quickly*]: Keep quiet.

DESIREE: I won't give you away if you tell me everything. That first
night, who lent you the makeup and the wrap?

LUCY [*laughs*]: I was so afraid back then.

DESIREE: But everything went all right, didn't it?

LUCY: It went very quickly.

DESIREE: Tell me.

LUCY: It's much simpler than you'd imagine, Fräulein.

DESIREE: Call me Desiree.

LUCY: I only use first names with the other people.

DESIREE: Do you know lots of other people already?

LUCY: I can't even count them.

DESIREE: Don't make me worm it out of you. How old are you?

LUCY: Eighteen.

DESIREE: That's good. You go with anyone at all?

LUCY: Yes.

DESIREE: You don't care what he looks like?

LUCY: I don't even look.

DESIREE: Very good. What if something happens to you?

LUCY: You can't have a baby, anyway.

DESIREE: Why can't you have a baby?

LUCY: Herr Freder told me how.

DESIREE: You make them pay a lot?

LUCY: Yesterday there was this guy—while he was sleeping, I looked in his wallet. I wanted to see who he was.

DESIREE: Fantastic. Who was he?

LUCY [*laughs*]: A boxer.

DESIREE [*abruptly*]: I'm going to go a bit of the way with you.

LUCY [*alarmed*]: Nobody will talk to me then.

DESIREE: I'll do my makeup like yours.

LUCY: But we mustn't walk side by side.

DESIREE: Don't worry. Some men like two girls at once.

LUCY: I didn't know that.

DESIREE: There are lots of things you still don't know. Just a minute, Lucy. I'll be ready in no time.

MARIE: You're going to change?

DESIREE [*laughs*]: I'm going with her.

MARIE: You've lost your mind.

DESIREE: It was never any use to me.

ALT: Come with me, Fräulein Lucy.

DESIREE [*laughs*]: You won't stop me.

MARIE: This is going to end in a prizefight.

DESIREE: I want to peddle my flesh.

MARIE: Daisy.

DESIREE [*imitating*]: Daisy. I want to peddle my flesh.

[DESIREE *goes into her room.*]

LUCY [*surprised*]: Peddle your flesh?

ALT: Come on.

LUCY: I don't peddle my flesh, not me.

ALT: Of course not.

LUCY: I won't let you insult me.

ALT: Bravo.

LUCY: Herr Freder will show her.

ALT: You go and complain to him.

LUCY: He jilted her.

[MARIE *goes into* DESIREE*'s room.*]

ALT: She can't get over him. Come with me, quick.

LUCY: But at the corner, you'll leave me on my own, doctor?

ALT: Don't worry.

[ALT *and* LUCY *exit.*]

SCENE 4

MARIE [*offstage*]: Come to your senses.

DESIREE [*offstage*]: Give me the key.

MARIE [*offstage*]: I won't consent to this madness.

[DESIREE *enters, runs through the room to the door.*]

DESIREE: How dare you.

[MARIE *follows* DESIREE, *barring the door.*]

MARIE: No.

DESIREE: You won't let me go?

MARIE: Daisy.

DESIREE: I'll scratch your face.

MARIE: Do what you want.

DESIREE: You're not my mother.

MARIE: I am not your mother.

[DESIREE *leaps on* MARIE.]

[MARIE *pushes* DESIREE *away*.]

MARIE: You'll have to kill me first.

DESIREE [*enraged*]: I wouldn't do you the pleasure.

MARIE: Daisy.

DESIREE: I want to peddle my flesh.

MARIE: I know.

DESIREE: You have no right.

MARIE: I have no right.

DESIREE: You're crazy, not me.

MARIE: I'm crazy, not you.

DESIREE: Let me go. I can't spend another night with you.

MARIE: We'll sleep apart. I'll make up my bed in here.

DESIREE: You bore me. You disgust me.

MARIE: Whatever you say.

DESIREE: I lust after strangers today, men as dirty as possible. I want a boxer too. Let me peddle my flesh. You're jealous, aren't you?

MARIE: Perhaps I am jealous.

DESIREE: You've gone out of your mind.

MARIE: Perhaps I have gone out of my mind.

DESIREE: You married man. [*Pauses*.]

MARIE [*tenderly*]: Daisy.

[DESIREE *is silent*.]

MARIE [*sits next to her*]: Little wild animal.

DESIREE: Give me my key.

MARIE: No.

DESIREE: I've never let anyone rob me of my freedom. The man who locks up his wife will be cheated on in no time.

MARIE: You'd dare cheat on me. Baby, I didn't know how wicked you can be.

[DESIREE *goes into her room.*]

[MARIE *remains seated, exhausted. She starts drinking. Then she goes into* DESIREE*'s room.*]

DESIREE [*offstage.*] Leave me alone.

MARIE [*offstage*]: I won't do anything.

DESIREE [*offstage*]: Give me back my key.

[MARIE *laughs, and returns with a blanket and a pillow; she makes up a bed on the chaise longue; she takes frequent drinks.*]

SCENE 5

[ALT *enters.*]

MARIE: She's in her room.

ALT: Calmer?

MARIE: Quite the contrary.

ALT: We can calm her down tomorrow.

MARIE: One for the road?

ALT: No thanks. Good night.

MARIE: Alt?

ALT: Yes?

MARIE [*after a pause*]: How far did you walk with Lucy?

ALT: Just downstairs—she ran off at once.

MARIE: She's very attractive. Alt.

ALT: Yes?

MARIE [*pauses*]: Good night.

ALT: Do you want to say something?

MARIE: I shouldn't have stopped her.

ALT: Don't be silly.

MARIE: I'm going to tell her she can go if she wants.

ALT: Keep calm. She'll sleep it off.

MARIE: She won't sleep all night.

ALT: Let her think it over.

MARIE: She sees herself as a victim.

ALT: That's how life works.

MARIE [*pauses*]: No one has the right to desert.

ALT [*firmly*]: No one has the right to desert.

MARIE: Don't shout at me like that.

ALT [*suddenly*]: I'll sleep here with you.

[MARIE *laughs.*]

ALT: I'm not interested in you.

MARIE: Don't you trust me?

ALT: Even less.

MARIE [*astonished*]: Alt?

ALT: She's recovered from more than one fit of depression.

MARIE: I haven't.

ALT: You haven't. She's known for a long time that everything always ends in disappointment.

MARIE: I haven't.

ALT: You haven't.

MARIE: You talk about her all the time.

ALT: You—

MARIE: What?

ALT: Everything's bottled up in you. Let things out.

MARIE: Show me the instruction manual.

ALT: All you need is to be casual. Be crueler to people, forget yourself, and you'll find yourself again.

MARIE: Amen.

ALT: That's masculine protest peeping out.

MARIE: Keep your ten commandments to yourself.

ALT: There were only four.

MARIE: You can't stand being contradicted. Your goodness is your desire to be in charge, same as Freder.

ALT: Freder?

MARIE: Desiree is right. You are two brothers who don't look alike. Go home and sleep tight.

ALT: Desiree's psychology—

MARIE: Her instinct makes her cleverer than either of us.

ALT: Fall in love with her again. Ask her forgiveness.

MARIE [*stares at him*]: I will ask her forgiveness.

ALT: From that moment you become her slave.

MARIE [*smiles*]: Perhaps.

ALT: She will abuse you.

MARIE: She's been abusing me for a long time now. No worries.

ALT: As you like.

MARIE: Sleep tight. Freder is here, in any case.

ALT: I don't trust him.

MARIE: We don't need a custodian.

ALT: Good night.

MARIE [*quickly*]: Alt.

ALT: Yes?

MARIE [*pause*]: Good night.

[ALT *exits.*]

[MARIE *goes to* DESIREE's *door.*]

MARIE: Open up, you stupid girl. Are you in bed already? Here's the key. I won't stand in your way. If you think something will come of it, go downstairs. Answer me. I'm putting the key on the floor, in front of the door—you only have to open it a crack. [*Pauses; speaks quietly.*] Forgive me, Daisy. [*Falls to her knees.*] Forgive me, Daisy. I was worried about you. Answer me! [*Beside herself.*] I don't even deserve an answer? [*Bangs on the door with her fists.*] I won't leave this spot until you answer me. If you don't open, I'll stay by this door all night.

SCENE 6

[DESIREE, *in a nightgown, opens the door, falls into* MARIE's *arms.*]

DESIREE: Kiss me.

MARIE: You.

[MARIE *kisses* DESIREE.]

DESIREE [*with great affection*]: Forgive me, Marion.

MARIE: You.

[MARIE *and* DESIREE *sit on the bed, pressed against one another.*]

DESIREE [*smiles*]: Let's die together.

MARIE: Don't die.

DESIREE: Help me, Marion.

MARIE [*sobbing*]: Don't die.

DESIREE: That's all I can do, little sister.

MARIE [*kisses* DESIREE]: I'll stay with you.

DESIREE: Let's die together. I know everything already.

MARIE: No one ever knows everything.

DESIREE: I already feel drugged. As if the oxygen mask were placed over my face. I hold you in my arms, as if in a mist.

MARIE: I'll carry you to your bed.

DESIREE: It's only one little step.

MARIE: Don't talk.

DESIREE: I'm already halfway to the other side. One little step. Do it, Marie. Pour the Veronal in my glass.

MARIE [*imploring*]: Not another word.

[MARIE *falls to her knees.*]

MARIE: Daisy.

DESIREE: Help me, mother, help me.

MARIE [*upset*]: Not another word, for pity's sake.

DESIREE [*more alert*]: Will you do it? I'm ready for it. I was in my bed, dreaming of you.

MARIE: We'll sit side by side and keep still.

DESIREE: How silly, to go on the streets!

MARIE [*desperate*]: It wasn't silly.

DESIREE: Thanks for holding me back.

MARIE [*almost entreating*]: We'll go down together. I'll go with you.

DESIREE [*smiles*]: I don't need the street any more. I don't need the boxer any more. Marion, you'll stay with me. [*Kisses* MARIE.] I dreamed that you would help me.

MARIE: Don't talk about that any more.

DESIREE: You called to me. You knocked on the door and woke me up. Say you'll do it. Say yes, even if you won't.

MARIE: Why do you keep torturing me?

DESIREE: Just say yes. It will comfort me.

MARIE [*quietly*]: Yes.

DESIREE, Thank you.

MARIE: I'm going to carry you to bed now.

DESIREE: Look into my eyes.

[MARIE *takes* DESIREE *in her arms.*]

MARIE: Come.

DESIREE: Beautiful, strong eyes.

[MARIE *begins to carry* DESIREE *toward her room.*]

MARIE: You are going to sleep now.

DESIREE: You're beautiful, Marion.

[DESIREE *suddenly embraces* MARIE.]

DESIREE: Forgive me.

MARIE: I'll sit beside you until you fall asleep.

MARIE [*offstage*]: Are you all right?

DESIREE [*offstage*]: I love you, Marion.

MARIE [*offstage*]: I'm putting out the light.

[*Dark in the next room.*]

MARIE: Sleep, baby.

DESIREE [*offstage, very quietly*]: I love you.

MARIE [*after a brief pause*]: Are you asleep?

[DESIREE *gives no answer.*]

SCENE 7

[FREDER *enters in shirtsleeves, goes to the open door of* DESIREE's *room.*]

FREDER: You're not asleep already, are you?

[MARIE *enters, closes the door.*]

MARIE: She's asleep.

FREDER: Are you tired too?

MARIE: Yes.

FREDER: So early?

[FREDER *pours a glass of wine.*]

MARIE: You shouldn't drink.

FREDER: We're not married yet.

MARIE: Stop, it's absurd.

FREDER: How long will it be absurd?

MARIE: You're confusing me with Lucy.

FREDER: Lucy is a creature of genius.

MARIE: So I've noticed.

FREDER: The only way you can get anywhere is with her sleepwalker's confidence. I envy her.

MARIE: You've brought her very far. How did you manage it?

FREDER: She did it. Not me.

MARIE: You know what I mean.

FREDER: I've never seen you so beautiful.

MARIE: You mustn't drink.

FREDER: One glass more or less. The footbath did me good. I'm up for anything again.

MARIE: Leave me alone.

FREDER: I can't sleep.

MARIE: But I'm tired.

FREDER: You're so inconsiderate.

MARIE [*exhausted*]: Give me a break.

FREDER: I've never seen you so beautiful.

MARIE: I can't stand on my feet.

FREDER: You're so pale, a man could be mad about you.

MARIE: I feel rotten.

FREDER: So do I.

MARIE: I'm worried about Daisy.

FREDER: What's wrong with Daisy?

MARIE: She wanted to be a streetwalker. I held her back. I shouldn't have.

FREDER: Daisy isn't made for the streets. Daisy has no resistance, and at the same time she has willpower. That blend of character traits is the unluckiest in the world.

MARIE: I worry about her.

FREDER: That blend leads to suicide.

MARIE: Shut up. You're the one who took away her will to live.

FREDER: When she ran away at seventeen? I only speeded up inevitable consequences.

MARIE: If only she had never met you.

FREDER [*laughs*]: You are all alive, thanks to me.

MARIE: You were dropped on your head.

FREDER: You fancy me too.

MARIE: I won't even answer that.

FREDER: You fancy me sharp as a knife.

[FREDER *approaches* MARIE.]

MARIE: Leave me alone.

FREDER: You smell blood. There's only one way out—marriage.

MARIE [*laughs*]: A fine way out.

FREDER: At the very last moment we'll opt to be middle-class. The only salvation when faced with catastrophe.

MARIE: I've already heard that from Desiree.

FREDER: She's more intelligent than you.

MARIE: Perhaps.

FREDER: And more perceptive. You don't live by your nerves. You still live by your instincts, like Lucy.

MARIE: We're both from Passau.

FREDER: You're what?

MARIE: That just popped into my head.

FREDER: I could make you go on the streets, like Lucy.

MARIE [*looks up*]: You're joking.

FREDER: You're a tramp. You just have to pick your beat. No matter which one.

MARIE: Are you done?

FREDER: No. You could be the hardest worker, twenty hours a day in the operating theater. You could become the mother of ten children. You could become the toughest of streetwalkers. All possibilities are dormant in you. Born under a lucky star, you are the very cliché of a young woman with full potential.

MARIE: I'm going to try one of those prospects.

FREDER: But to be nothing, you're incapable of that. It is destroying you.

MARIE: I'll think about it.

FREDER: I'm not joking. Opt for a moral career, and it'll make you the perfect paragon.

MARIE: I'll think about that too.

FREDER: I'm not joking.

MARIE: You won't get around me.

FREDER: I only want to help you.

MARIE: Help your Lucy instead.

FREDER: She doesn't need me anymore. Lucy only needed to be awakened.

MARIE: Let me go on sleeping.

FREDER: That's not what you want.

MARIE: Who told you that?

FREDER: I don't have elephant skin. You want to wake up. So long as you had Boysie, you were sleeping soundly.

MARIE: Leave him out of it.

FREDER: Now you have to search. That means staying awake. But anyone who wakes up too late dies of it.

MARIE: Will you leave me alone at last?

FREDER: I repeat my proposal, earnest as can be.

MARIE: I'm already married.

FREDER: To Daisy?

MARIE: To Daisy.

FREDER: You'll soon be a widow.

[MARIE *leaps up*.]

MARIE: I loathe you.

FREDER: At last.

MARIE: I hate you.

FREDER: That's a declaration of love in itself.

MARIE: I could kill you.

FREDER: Bravo. Thalassa! Thalassa!

MARIE [*furious*]: You haven't caught me yet.

FREDER: You're giving up?

MARIE: You don't know me well.

FREDER: But I already have you.

MARIE: Don't you dare.

FREDER: Without touching you, I have you.

MARIE: You're dreaming.

FREDER: We'll dream together.

MARIE: I'd rather kill myself.

FREDER: I horrify you that much?

MARIE: I loathe you.

FREDER: You've said that already.

MARIE: I hate you.

FREDER: All right.

MARIE: Get out of this room.

FREDER: This ferocity suits you even better. Now you sport primary colors.

MARIE: I'm the one who'll leave, if you don't.

FREDER: Try.

MARIE: You want me to go stark raving mad?

FREDER: Yes.

[MARIE *runs to the door.*]

MARIE: I can't stand it.

FREDER: The lights are out in the vestibule.

MARIE: I'm going to Frau Schimmelbrot's.

FREDER: She'll thank you.

MARIE [*erupting*]: I can't stand you anymore.

FREDER: You're caught.

MARIE: Shut up or I'll strangle you.

FREDER: I'm not moving.

MARIE: And if I plead with you?

FREDER: Get on your knees.

MARIE: Then you'll leave me alone?

FREDER: On your knees.

[MARIE *falls to her knees.*]

MARIE: Leave me alone. I beg of you.

FREDER: Say the Lord's Prayer.

MARIE: God in heaven, I'm going insane.

FREDER: Our Father, Which art in heaven—

MARIE: I can't stand it.

FREDER: Give us this day our daily bread—

[MARIE *throws herself on* FREDER.]

MARIE: Get out.

[FREDER *holds* MARIE *tight.*]

FREDER: Forgive us our trespasses . . .

MARIE: Get out.

FREDER: As we forgive those—

[FREDER *kisses* MARIE.]

FREDER: You've never been so beautiful.

[MARIE *tries to get loose.*]

MARIE: I'm going to strangle you.

FREDER: Your rage is contagious.

MARIE: Let go of me.

[FREDER *kisses* MARIE.]

FREDER: After the Lord's Prayer, one can die in peace.

MARIE: I'm going to scream.

[FREDER *and* MARIE *both fall on the bed.* MARIE *manages to get free and runs into* DESIREE*'s room.* FREDER *runs after her.*]

FREDER: That won't help you.

[FREDER *enters* DESIREE*'s room.*]

[*Pause.*]

[MARIE *returns and sinks onto a chair.* FREDER *appears in the doorway a moment later.*]

MARIE [*quietly*]: Is it too late?

FREDER: Too late.

MARIE: What can we do for her?

FREDER: Nothing.

MARIE: I have to get Alt.

FREDER: Too late.

MARIE: A minute ago she was still with me. She was calling me a fool . . .

FREDER: That's the fate of survivors.

MARIE: She must have taken the Veronal before she came to me. It acts so quickly.

FREDER: It depends on the amount.

MARIE [*pauses*]: We should send for a doctor.

FREDER: I'm satisfied.

MARIE: You never know.

FREDER: What's the point?

MARIE: What's the point?

FREDER: She'll start all over again.

MARIE: What's the point?

FREDER: Was she lively?

MARIE: She was very tired.

FREDER: Was she happy?

MARIE [*pauses*]: The door was closed when I wanted to get in to her. I had to make a racket before she could hear me.

FREDER: She was already far gone.

MARIE: It acts so quickly.

FREDER: It depends on the amount.

MARIE: How could she have got so much?

FREDER [*simply*]: I got it for her.

MARIE [*quietly*]: You horrify me.

FREDER: You want me to leave the room?

MARIE [*quickly*]: No.

FREDER: You wanted to be alone.

MARIE [*quietly*]: Murderer.

[FREDER *is silent.*]

MARIE: Why did you get her Veronal?

FREDER: Otherwise she probably would have drowned herself.

MARIE: She would have had time to come to her senses.

FREDER: Because the water is cold?

MARIE: Because a second later, she'd regret it.

FREDER: She was with you later, and she didn't regret it.

MARIE [*after a pause*]: What should we do?

FREDER: She asked me for it.

MARIE: Murderer.

FREDER: Your obsession.

MARIE: Little birdie, my little sister.

FREDER: I'll leave you alone.

MARIE: Don't take a step.

FREDER: I don't like funeral orations.

MARIE: We can be quiet too. [*Pauses.*]

[FREDER *drinks.*]

MARIE [*quietly*]: Me too. [*Pauses.*] Now you've got me where you want me.

FREDER: Where is that?

MARIE: Don't pretend.

FREDER: You're imagining things.

MARIE: Drink.[*Points to* DESIREE's *door.*] Is the door shut tight?

FREDER: It embarrasses you?

MARIE: Drink.

FREDER: She won't hear us, in any case.

MARIE [*going to the door*]: It's closed.

FREDER: You want to go to bed?

MARIE: You know it well enough.

FREDER: I don't.

MARIE: I'll whisper in your ear.

FREDER [*dodging* MARIE]: Nobody's listening.

MARIE: Don't run away.

FREDER: Go on, say it.

MARIE [*chasing* FREDER]: Are you afraid of me?

FREDER: I don't understand.

MARIE: I'm not going to bite your ear.

FREDER [*catching* MARIE]: Now you're the one losing your mind.

MARIE: Could be.

FREDER: I'd better go. I'll send for a doctor.

MARIE: Get on your knees.

FREDER: Good night.

MARIE: On your knees.

FREDER: Marie.

MARIE: You won't get out of here with a Lord's Prayer.

FREDER: What do you want?

MARIE: Sit up and beg. Doggy'll get a treat. Sit up and beg.

FREDER: You're weird.

MARIE: I'm beautiful.

FREDER: Marie.

MARIE: I've never been so beautiful.

FREDER: Quiet.

MARIE: I haven't forgotten your words.

FREDER: There's a dead woman next door.

MARIE: Nothing matters any more.

FREDER: There's a dead woman next door.

MARIE: Your obsession. Drink.

[MARIE *drinks.*]

FREDER: You're stark raving mad.

MARIE: That makes me much more desirable. Do you want to take me?

FREDER: Stop playing games.

MARIE: Thalassa! Thalassa!

FREDER: I'm out of my mind.

MARIE: Thalassa! Thalassa!

FREDER [*savagely*]: Stop playing around.

[FREDER *chases* MARIE.]

MARIE [*laughs*]: Catch me.

[*Chase.*]

MARIE: Catch me. I loathe you. I hate you.

[FREDER *catches* MARIE.]

FREDER: Not another word.

MARIE [*laughing even harder*]: Go on, drink.

FREDER: I warn you.

MARIE: You haven't had enough to drink.

[FREDER *moves to the door.*]

FREDER: Before I lose my mind completely—

MARIE: The lights are out in the vestibule.

FREDER: I'm leaving.

MARIE: You're going to knock over a chair.

FREDER: There's no harm in that.

MARIE: Frau Schimmelbrot will thank you.

FREDER: This is where the harm is.

MARIE: Your obsession.

FREDER: I can't put up with you any longer.

MARIE: Caught.

[FREDER *tears* MARIE*'s blouse.*]

MARIE: I'm going to bed.

FREDER: Marie.

MARIE [*as she laughs*]: I hate you. I loathe you. Do you give up?

FREDER: I won't say another word.

MARIE: Our Father, Which art in—

FREDER [*furious*]: Shut up.

MARIE: Forgive us our trespasses—

[FREDER *throws himself on* MARIE.]

MARIE [*still laughing.*] Is that all? Boysie can do that too.

[MARIE *pulls loose.*]

MARIE: As we forgive—

[FREDER *chases* MARIE.]

FREDER: I'll catch you.

MARIE: Catch me.

FREDER: God forgive us.

[FREDER *chases* MARIE.]

MARIE: Who is God?

[MARIE *pulls loose.*]

MARIE: You're tearing my pretty pajamas. Come on, Boysie, come on.

FREDER [*beside himself*]: I'm not your Boysie. I've lost a shoe.

MARIE: Run, Boysie, run.

FREDER: No more running.

MARIE: Boysie knows how to kiss too. Better than you.

[MARIE *pulls loose.*]

MARIE: You're hurting me. He knows how to bite too. The throat, Boysie.

FREDER: I'm not your Boysie.

MARIE: You're going to knock over the table.

[FREDER *throws* MARIE *on the bed.*]

MARIE: Drink some more first. You haven't had enough to drink.

FREDER: I've stopped drinking.

MARIE: Put out the light.

[MARIE *tries to pull loose.*]

FREDER [*beside himself*]: Now stay here.

MARIE: I like you. You're strong. Put out the light.

[MARIE *runs away.*]

FREDER: I don't give a damn about the light. Stand still.

[MARIE *puts out the light.*]
[*In the dark.*]

MARIE: Over here, over here, over here.

FREDER: Try to get away from me again.

MARIE: I won't get away from you. You're strong.

FREDER: Marie.

MARIE [*from the bottom of her heart*]: Kill me. Kill me.

[MARIE *screams.*]
[*Curtain.*]

In the earliest performances, the general consensus was that the ending was too violent, so Bruckner rewrote the end of the play.

[*End 2*]

After MARIE: We can be quiet too. [*Pauses.*]

[FREDER *drinks.*]

MARIE: My little sister.

FREDER: We should send for a doctor, you're right.

MARIE [*quickly*]: Don't go away.

FREDER: Besides, you're afraid of me—

MARIE: I'm more afraid of being alone now.

FREDER: More afraid than of me—is that possible?

MARIE: Go on, drink.

[FREDER *goes to the table, drinks.*]

MARIE [*quietly*]: Me too.

[FREDER *pours* MARIE *a glass, and she empties it.*]

MARIE: What's to become of me?

FREDER: Asking the question means knowing the answer.

[MARIE *looks at* FREDER.]

FREDER: The answer is: go on living, one way or another.

MARIE: Go on living—

FREDER: Join the middle class when the time comes. With your eyes wide open.

MARIE: When I think of the dead girl.

FREDER: You were born and fated to be middle-class. For you're incapable of suicide, you wouldn't manage it, plain and simple.

MARIE [*nods*]: I couldn't.

FREDER: How many times these last few days did you make up your mind? It didn't happen, plain and simple.

MARIE: Incapable, plain and simple.

FREDER: Surprising as it is, this is proof that even the perfect paragon has her limits. For my part, I want my needs taken care of. I don't like to work. And that, you see, has no limits. You, on the contrary, like nothing better than working. So we complement one another and make a perfect couple.

[MARIE *stares at* FREDER *in despair.*]

FREDER: It's inevitable.

[FREDER *sits at the table and starts to eat.*]

MARIE [*quietly*]: Help me.

FREDER [*his mouth full*]: All you women come to me, one way or another. Didn't I say that before? But some things have to be repeated over and over again before they come true. If it weren't for me, you couldn't live. Without a man to hold on to, you'd lose your mind.

MARIE: Help me.

FREDER: Eat. Life goes on.

[MARIE *begins to sob.*]

FREDER: You should eat something.

[MARIE, *in tears, reaches out for the food.*]
[*Curtain.*]

Criminals

✦ *A Play in Three Acts* ✦

CHARACTERS

FRAU VON WIEG

OTTFRIED ⎱
       ⎰ children of FRAU VON WIEG
LISELOTTE ⎱

DIETRICH VON WIEG, brother-in-law of FRAU VON WIEG

OLGA NAGERLE, a secretary

KUMMERER, a university student

GUSTAV TUNICHTGUT, a waiter

ALFRED FISCHAU

[FRAU FISCHAU, mother of ALRED FISCHAU (nonspeaking character)]

FRAU BERLESSEN

JOSEF ⎱
    ⎰ sons of FRAU BERLESSEN
FRANK ⎱

ERNESTINE PUSCHEK, a cook

MIMI ZERL, a housemaid

KARLA KUDELKA, a barmaid

KAKS, a hairdresser

In addition, in act I:

2 POLICE INSPECTORS

CORONER

In addition, in act II:

4 PRESIDING JUDGES

SEVERAL ADDITIONAL JUDGES

YOUNGER JUDGE

OLDER JUDGE

4 DEFENSE COUNSELS

3 PUBLIC PROSECUTORS

IMMANUEL SCHIMMELWEIS

COURT OFFICER

CLERK OF THE COURT

In addition, in act III:

CARLA KOCH, a housemaid

DEFENSE COUNSEL

BEN SIM, a boxer

WAITER

A WOMAN

2 POLICE INSPECTORS

2 LADIES

FISTELKREUZ, a custodian

A YOUNG MAN

The gradual lighting at the beginnings and the gradual darkening at the endings of scenes are part of the concept of the three-level stage construction. The author did not intend any stylization, even though the simultaneous acting in all scenes at the end of acts might suggest it. The full, absolutely realistic performance in even the briefest scene he leaves to the conscience of the director.

ACT I

Apartment house

Top level

FRAU VON WIEG*'s room* (area 1)

OLGA NAGERLE*'s room* (area 2)

GUSTAV TUNICHTGUT*'s room* (area 3)

Middle level

ALFRED FISCHAU*'s room* (area 4)

FRAU BERLESSEN*'s living room* (area 5)

Kitchen (area 6)

Bottom level

Backroom of KARLA KUDELKA*'s bar* (area 7)

Vertical cross-section through three levels

Top	Area 1 FRAU VON WIEG's room	Area 2 OLGA NAGERLE's room	Area 3 GUSTAV TUNICHTGUT's room
Middle	Area 4 ALFRED FISCHAU's room	Area 5 FRAU BERLESSEN's living room	Area 6 Kitchen
Bottom		Area 7 Backroom of KARLA KUDELKA's bar	

[Areas 1–3 *on the upper level will be lit at the beginning.*]

[Area 1, FRAU VON WIEG*'s room:* FRAU VON WIEG, *alone, opens the bottom drawer of a dresser and carefully takes out a jewel box, which she opens.*]

[Area 2, OLGA NAGERLE*'s room:* OLGA, *twenty-one years old, alone, is working at a typewriter; she interrupts herself now and again, stares into space, then goes on typing.*]

[Area 3, *the waiter* GUSTAV TUNICHTGUT*'s room:* TUNICHTGUT, *alone, shaving; the gramophone beside him is playing a fox-trot.*]

[*Pause.*]

[TUNICHTGUT *stamps on the floor.*]

[Area 6, *the kitchen, lights up.*]

[Area 6, the kitchen: ERNESTINE PUSCHEK, *the cook, leaves the kitchen range, stands on a chair, and knocks on the ceiling.*]

[TUNICHTGUT *laughs.*]

[ERNESTINE *laughs and sings along with the fox-trot.*]

[Area 6, *the kitchen, goes dark.*]

[OLGA *utters a faint cry, pulls herself together, and goes on typing.*]

[Area 2, OLGA*'s room, goes dark.*]

TUNICHTGUT [*laughs*]: Women are all the same. Just give 'em a pat on the behind. [*Goes on shaving.*]

[Area 3, TUNICHTGUT*'s room, goes dark.*]

[Area 1, FRAU VON WIEG*'s room, lights up again.*]

FRAU VON WIEG [*rummaging in the jewel box*]: No doubt about it. There's less than there was.

[*A knock at the door.*]

[FRAU VON WIEG *is alarmed, puts away the box.*]

[OTTFRIED, *her son, comes in.*]

FRAU VON WIEG: You frightened me.

OTTFRIED: I can't imagine why.

FRAU VON WIEG: No kiss for me?

OTTFRIED: What were you hiding there?

FRAU VON WIEG: Don't be silly.

OTTFRIED: Show me, Mother.

FRAU VON WIEG: Will you leave it alone?

OTTFRIED: So you keep secrets from me?

FRAU VON WIEG: So long as there are still secrets to be kept.

OTTFRIED: That's what Liselotte says too.

FRAU VON WIEG: That ungrateful brat. Have you had your lesson?

OTTFRIED: Liselotte claims that you have a secret hoard.

FRAU VON WIEG: She was always romantically inclined.

OTTFRIED: You're wrong there.

FRAU VON WIEG: When we still had our property, she used to dream that the chauffeur would have an accident so that she could care for him.

OTTFRIED: You call that romantic? You're the only romantic around here.

FRAU VON WIEG: If you only knew.

OTTFRIED [*suddenly*]: What?

FRAU VON WIEG: What your mother has gone through for your sake.

OTTFRIED: Spit it out.

FRAU VON WIEG: I don't owe you an accounting.

OTTFRIED: All the same, we wonder where you get your money.

FRAU VON WIEG: You both have to take your exams. When is Liselotte getting her diploma?

OTTFRIED: She can tell you better than I can.

FRAU VON WIEG: As soon as Liselotte has her diploma, I'll find her her first student.

OTTFRIED: That'll make her happy.

FRAU VON WIEG: Frau von Beningsen wants her daughter to take piano lessons. She promised me. And the Berlessens downstairs can't play the piano.

OTTFRIED: A wide field. Can you give me a hundred marks?

FRAU VON WIEG: What for?

OTTFRIED: I haven't paid Professor Hahn yet.

FRAU VON WIEG: Why an intelligent young man has to have special tutoring at night . . .

OTTFRIED: Given my high-class education . . .

FRAU VON WIEG: So that's my fault too.

OTTFRIED: Till the day he died, Father kept saying it was beneath our dignity to know the meaning of money.

FRAU VON WIEG: He was a member of the Upper Chamber.

OTTFRIED: Which is why we have to go begging these days.

FRAU VON WIEG [*sharp*]: Who goes begging?

OTTFRIED: You.

FRAU VON WIEG: Get out of here, you lout.

OTTFRIED: How else do you get your money?

FRAU VON WIEG: We have our pension.

[OTTFRIED *laughs*.]

FRAU VON WIEG: You know that we own valuable possessions, which I have to sell one by one, until your studies are finished.

OTTFRIED: Which is why we had to end up in this dump. Don't overtax your strength.

FRAU VON WIEG: What do you really want?

OTTFRIED: A hundred marks.

FRAU VON WIEG: For Professor Hahn?

OTTFRIED: Why else?

FRAU VON WIEG: Tell him to come to me. I still don't know what he looks like.

OTTFRIED: That costs extra.

FRAU VON WIEG: Then I give up. You can have the hundred marks tomorrow.

OTTFRIED: And where are you going to get it?

FRAU VON WIEG: Mind your own business. Where will you be?

OTTFRIED: Cramming. That a one-time baronial landowner has to sit for exams is incredible.

FRAU VON WIEG: Nothing should be impossible for you.

OTTFRIED: That's the sort of sweet talk that made me what I am today.

FRAU VON WIEG: Come, give me a kiss first.

OTTFRIED: That too.

FRAU VON WIEG: What do you mean?

OTTFRIED: Did you prepare me for life?

FRAU VON WIEG: You ungrateful lout. I don't sleep at night because of you.

OTTFRIED [*quickly*]: Then what's the secret?

FRAU VON WIEG: Get out of my sight.

OTTFRIED [*laughs*]: As you like. Don't forget the hundred marks, though.

[OTTFRIED *exits.*]

[FRAU VON WIEG *locks the door behind* OTTFRIED *and takes out the jewel box again.*]

[*The stage goes dark.*]

[*Area 4,* ALFRED FISCHAU'*s room, lights up.*]

[FRAU BERLESSEN *enters.*]

FRAU BERLESSEN [*still very well preserved*]: Alfred Fischau.

ALFRED [*quietly*]: You won't take me seriously.

FRAU BERLESSEN: I have two grown sons. Josef is even older than you.

ALFRED: I have no money. That is my whole trouble.

FRAU BERLESSEN: You're a child. [*Strokes the back of* ALFRED'*s hand.*]

[ALFRED *seizes* FRAU BERLESSEN'*s hand and kisses it passionately.*]

[FRAU BERLESSEN *smiles and draws her hand away.*]

ALFRED [*worried*]: Are you angry with me?

FRAU BERLESSEN: Are you going to the opera tonight?

ALFRED: You think I'm a fool?

FRAU BERLESSEN: Perhaps.

ALFRED: Because I love you, because I'm young and have no money.

FRAU BERLESSEN: Stop going on about money.

ALFRED: My mom keeps me on short commons, and I earn too little as a volunteer. But I know how I can get some. We're meant for one another.

FRAU BERLESSEN: How can you be so sure of that?

ALFRED: I only have to see how unhappy you are with your husband. The walls have ears.

FRAU BERLESSEN: You eavesdrop?

ALFRED: When he yells at you, a deaf man could hear it.

FRAU BERLESSEN: It's his prerogative as father of the family.

ALFRED: But you don't look like the mother of a family.

FRAU BERLESSEN: That's no compliment.

ALFRED: Your sons are grown. One of them doesn't even live here anymore.

FRAU BERLESSEN: What about Frank?

ALFRED: I am his best friend. But I don't understand him.

FRAU BERLESSEN: Neither do I.

ALFRED: You couldn't do anything to change him. You have control only over your own life.

FRAU BERLESSEN: So you don't see Frank very often?

ALFRED: And if you make a mess of it, it'll be your own fault.

FRAU BERLESSEN: I took you into this house for Frank's sake. You've been friends from childhood.

ALFRED: The only unhappy endings when a woman is a couple of months older are in plays.

FRAU BERLESSEN [*laughs*]: A couple of months? Give me your hand and look me in the face.

ALFRED: Nothing will make me change my mind. You won't put me off with half measures.

FRAU BERLESSEN [*smiles*]: You want to have it all.

ALFRED: All.

[JOSEF *enters*.]

JOSEF: So here you are?

FRAU BERLESSEN [*embarrassed*]: Waiting for you to show up at last.

ALFRED: Good morning, Herr Berlessen.

JOSEF: Good morning, young man.

FRAU BERLESSEN: Herr Fischau wanted to lend me a book. Where have you been?

[JOSEF *looks behind her*.]

FRAU BERLESSEN: You'll have some tea anyway.

[FRAU BERLESSEN *hurries out.*]

ALFRED: Won't you sit down?

JOSEF: Let me give you a piece of advice. Leave my mother alone.

ALFRED [*startled*]: Herr Berlessen!

JOSEF: Don't you think I've got eyes in my head? Even if I do come round here less frequently.

ALFRED: How dare you. Your own mother.

JOSEF: Mainly I find it unaesthetic. The woman is forty years old.

ALFRED: Allow me to withdraw.

JOSEF: You are in your own room. But I'll take advantage of the opportunity. Find another one on the double.

ALFRED: So far as I know—

JOSEF: I am not master of the house. Shall I tell my father that he has a rival?

ALFRED: You may do whatever you please.

[ALFRED *is about to go.*]

JOSEF: Stay here.

ALFRED: I'm not used to this.

JOSEF: Stay here.

ALFRED [*upset*]: Nobody can order me around.

JOSEF: Down, boy! You'd like to make a scandal, wouldn't you? A catastrophe, to cover up your smutty intentions.

ALFRED: If she weren't in the next room—

JOSEF: Then you'd shoot me down—

ALFRED: —like a hyena.

JOSEF: That sounds much better.

ALFRED: Clear the hell out of here! This is my room.

JOSEF [*lays hands on an exercise book lying on the desk; reads*]: "The longing of your soul incarnate in your limbs, as they entwine my deeply besotted heart."

ALFRED [*beside himself, grabs the book from him*]: You monster.

JOSEF: A poem to my mother?

ALFRED [*clenches his fists*]: I'm going to forget myself.

JOSEF: Think of the longing in the limbs.

ALFRED: You could sully the purest feeling. Everything turns rotten as soon as you look at it.

JOSEF: With the eyes of reality.

ALFRED: You call your money reality. Because you waste it on whores, while your family here—

JOSEF: Has to rent rooms?

ALFRED: My mother sends the rent every month. And I know from Frank that the money is needed.

JOSEF: If a person has no other way of earning it.

ALFRED: With your clean hands—I spit on that money.

JOSEF: I haven't offered you any yet. We have that in common as well.

ALFRED: I prefer having nothing in common with you.

JOSEF: Keep that phrase on hand until you've brought it to a member of Parliament. Meanwhile you can look for a woman somewhere else, you and your besotted heart.

ALFRED: Get out.

JOSEF: One floor down for instance. In the beer parlor. I'll lend you the ten marks.

[ALFRED *flings himself at* JOSEF *and hits him in the face.*]

JOSEF [*shakes loose from* ALFRED]: Idiot.

ALFRED [*drops onto a chair*]: I can't go on living.

[JOSEF *exits.*]

[*The stage goes dark.*]

[*Area 2,* OLGA's *room, lights up.*]

[OLGA *at the typewriter.*]

[ERNESTINE *enters.*]

ERNESTINE: You're going to stunt the kid with all that banging.

OLGA [*smiles*]: Don't worry.

ERNESTINE: I have a liter of milk here. Pains bad?

OLGA: If only I weren't so tired.

ERNESTINE: You'll end up having a cripple.

OLGA: Are we supposed to starve?

ERNESTINE: You had to go and marry a PhD, who can't earn a penny.

OLGA [*suddenly*]: I have to work. [*Goes on typing.*]

ERNESTINE: You're making us deaf, me and the kid. I'll feed you till the kid's born.

OLGA: What about the rent? And all the rest?

ERNESTINE: I'll feed your PhD too. Tonight they're having rabbit stew.

OLGA: We can't go on living off charity for long. I'll figure a way out. [*Goes on typing.*]

ERNESTINE [*tears* OLGA's *hands away from the typewriter*]: I won't take a cripple.

OLGA: Then I'll keep it.

ERNESTINE: Silly girl.

[ERNESTINE *kisses* OLGA *quickly*.]

OLGA: You're hurting me, Frau Puschek.

ERNESTINE: Stop making that racket.

OLGA: I have to type twelve pages today.

ERNESTINE: You're hammering coffin nails for my kid. Leave off.

OLGA [*laughs*]: You're crazy.

ERNESTINE: In a month's time it'll be born. Then you can type as much as you want. Only it has to be healthy when I get it. And nobody must know about it. Let me listen to its little heart. [*Holds her ear to* OLGA*'s belly*.] I hear it, I hear it. [*Strokes* OLGA*'s legs*.] You're my tootsy-wootsy, my sweet piggy-wiggy, I'll treat you right, I swear to you in your mother's belly. [*Rises, serious and calm*.] I'm not a complete human being, you know.

OLGA: Why do you want a child so badly?

ERNESTINE: I'm not a woman, 'cause I can't have one myself. And somebody like you has one and wants to get an abortion.

OLGA: When a person has nothing to eat.

ERNESTINE: You should thank God I came along in time.

OLGA [*depressed*]: It's a pity.

ERNESTINE [*quickly*]: A deal's a deal.

OLGA: I haven't the right to love it, because I can't keep it. And yet I do love it.

ERNESTINE: A deal's a deal. And nobody must ever know.

OLGA: I'll like to drown myself.

ERNESTINE: Let me have the kid first.

[ERNESTINE *exits.*]

[OLGA *goes on typing.*]

[*The stage goes dark.*]

[*Area 3, room of the waiter* TUNICHTGUT, *lights up.*]

[TUNICHTGUT *is finishing his toilette.*]

[ERNESTINE *enters and looks on.*]

TUNICHTGUT: Would my lady care to take a seat?

ERNESTINE [*laughs*]: You old smoothie.

TUNICHTGUT: Out of consideration for our offspring.

ERNESTINE: I'll pop it out like an alley cat. Don't you worry about that.

TUNICHTGUT: Wouldn't think it to look at you.

ERNESTINE [*affectionately*]: As if you'd see anything with your fish eyes.

TUNICHTGUT: But everybody who hears about it is surprised.

ERNESTINE: I don't let myself go.

TUNICHTGUT: Let me see.

ERNESTINE [*extricates herself, laughing*]: Till the kid is born don't even think about it.

TUNICHTGUT: Do I have to wait a whole month?

ERNESTINE: That's the least a father can do for his child.

TUNICHTGUT: It won't hurt him, dummy.

ERNESTINE: How do you know? It would be disgusting, Gustav.

TUNICHTGUT: Fiddle-dee-dee. [*Kisses her.*]

ERNESTINE: That's enough.

TUNICHTGUT [*half-joking*]: I'm warning you, Tinchen.

ERNESTINE: Get a grip. I said no.

TUNICHTGUT: I can't survive on reduced rations.

ERNESTINE: It's rabbit stew today.

TUNICHTGUT: Not again. Don't say I didn't warn you.

ERNESTINE [*suspiciously*]: Why are you getting all dolled up?

TUNICHTGUT: When I'm with my missus—

ERNESTINE: Who's a missus?

TUNICHTGUT: You are.

ERNESTINE: I'm not your missus.

TUNICHTGUT: A manner of speaking. With a kid at your breast.

ERNESTINE: I don't want to be a missus. I don't want you cheating on me.

TUNICHTGUT: Don't get so excited.

ERNESTINE: I don't give a damn about marriage. I can take care of myself. But you'd better not have somebody else.

TUNICHTGUT: Can't a man have his joke?

ERNESTINE: I can see your joke a mile off.

TUNICHTGUT: We're done then.

ERNESTINE: Don't you care that you're going to be a father?

TUNICHTGUT: Let's not overdo it.

ERNESTINE: Isn't there something sacred in my giving you a child—

TUNICHTGUT: I wouldn't say that.

ERNESTINE: —and won't it unite us forever?

TUNICHTGUT: I don't like to talk about it. You know that.

ERNESTINE: You like to use your tongue a different way, right? Swear to me that you've never cheated on me.

TUNICHTGUT: Now it's getting embarrassing.

ERNESTINE: Swear it, Gustav, or else I don't know what I'll do to the kid.

TUNICHTGUT: Just don't lose your head.

ERNESTINE: So you won't swear.

TUNICHTGUT: If you absolutely insist—

ERNESTINE: On the head of our child.

TUNICHTGUT: Now stop it.

ERNESTINE: Swear.

TUNICHTGUT [*laughs*]: I swear. My lady is in a foul temper today.

ERNESTINE: And don't you turn me into a missus. I won't let you cheat on me.

TUNICHTGUT: Drop it.

ERNESTINE: That's not why a woman bears a child. It can make a woman drop dead, get me?

TUNICHTGUT: Not a woman like you. I'm not worried.

ERNESTINE: Don't be so sure. [*Suddenly.*] Why did you tip your hat to the Kudelka woman?

TUNICHTGUT [*acts surprised*]: The Kudelka woman?

ERNESTINE: Yesterday on the stairs. I saw you do it.

TUNICHTGUT: Are you spying on me?

ERNESTINE: Since when do you know her?

TUNICHTGUT: I once got a bottle of beer from her bar.

ERNESTINE: And you tip your hat to her?

TUNICHTGUT: After all she is a lady. [*Laughs.*]

ERNESTINE: She's a barmaid, who pulls taps in the bedroom too.

TUNICHTGUT [*laughs*]: You're a filthy swine.

ERNESTINE: So do you know her more intimately?

TUNICHTGUT: What do you care?

ERNESTINE: Is that why you're dolling yourself up—for the Kudelka woman?

TUNICHTGUT: Don't be ridiculous.

ERNESTINE: Swear it.

TUNICHTGUT: Not again.

ERNESTINE: Because you stand up for that creature. Or are you after her money?

TUNICHTGUT: What do I care about her money?

ERNESTINE: It's the wages of sin.

TUNICHTGUT: I'm just being a gentleman.

ERNESTINE: You doll yourself up so the women will come after you. You'd better not look at a single one of them.

TUNICHTGUT: I only have eyes for you, my Goldilocks.

ERNESTINE: Say it again.

[TUNICHTGUT *kisses* ERNESTINE.]

ERNESTINE [*fondly*]: Maybe I'll lie down a bit—

TUNICHTGUT: That's right.

ERNESTINE: —till nightfall. Meanwhile you go and get a breath of air.

TUNICHTGUT: Do you have to go downstairs?

ERNESTINE: You old smoothie. [*Kisses* TUNICHTGUT.] The smart way you twirl your moustache.

TUNICHTGUT: Style is everything in life, my lady.

ERNESTINE [*laughs*]: Leave me in peace with your highbrow talk.

TUNICHTGUT: Make sure there's a glass of beer at supper.

ERNESTINE [*leaning on* TUNICHTGUT]: I'm very happy, Gustav.

[*The stage goes dark.*]

[*Area 1,* FRAU VON WIEG'*s room, lights up.*]

[FRAU VON WIEG; LISELOTTE, *her daughter, age 20.*]

LISELOTTE [*laughs*]: You can do magic, Mama.

FRAU VON WIEG: Nevertheless, I wonder how you manage to buy so much finery.

LISELOTTE: I know how to make money go a long way.

FRAU VON WIEG: You shouldn't color your lips so much, Liesl.

LISELOTTE: All the girls are doing it now.

FRAU VON WIEG: It looks dreadful.

LISELOTTE: Should I be a wallflower?

FRAU VON WIEG: A person can't even give you a kiss.

LISELOTTE: Nowadays young men don't put any stock in kisses.

FRAU VON WIEG [*laughs*]: But what about your mother? It's not bright colors that matter, but the fundamentals.

LISELOTTE: What do you mean?

FRAU VON WIEG: The fundamentals. I am trying to draw out what is hidden deep inside you. Everything else will come by itself.

LISELOTTE: Speaking of funds—where do you get the money?

FRAU VON WIEG: What money?

LISELOTTE: That you give us. For three years we've been swimming in money.

FRAU VON WIEG: Look around.

LISELOTTE: Not you. But we children. One has to hand it to you.

FRAU VON WIEG [*beaming*]: I don't want anything else from life.

LISELOTTE: Probably things will get better for you too. Uncle Dietrich is back.

FRAU VON WIEG [*turns pale*]: Uncle Dietrich is back.

LISELOTTE: Last night.

FRAU VON WIEG: He got back last night?

LISELOTTE: He walked right past me. [*Laughs.*] I must have changed a lot.

FRAU VON WIEG: Why must you have changed a lot?

LISELOTTE: Because he didn't recognize me. He walked right past me close up and even stared at me. He seems to have liked what he saw. What's wrong with you?

FRAU VON WIEG [*rises*]: Nothing. What are you doing tonight?

LISELOTTE: I'll be at Hermine's. Chamber music. You know. [*Hesitant.*] Would you like to come with?

FRAU VON WIEG: No.

LISELOTTE: We're playing Brahms's piano quintet today.

FRAU VON WIEG: Then shouldn't you be going?

LISELOTTE [*leaps at the chance*]: Of course, mama.

FRAU VON WIEG: Don't waste time. [*Suddenly.*] Why didn't you speak to Uncle Dietrich?

LISELOTTE: I—wasn't alone.

FRAU VON WIEG [*mechanically*]: You weren't alone?

LISELOTTE: With a girlfriend of Hermine's. She's studying the cello.

FRAU VON WIEG: You should have spoken to him all the same.

LISELOTTE: He'll pay us a visit.

FRAU VON WIEG: He'll pay us a visit. [*Hastily.*] Well, then, get going.

LISELOTTE [*observes her*]: Is there something wrong with Uncle Dietrich coming back?

FRAU VON WIEG [*sharply*]: What do you mean?

LISELOTTE: I'm just thinking. He must have got very rich?

FRAU VON WIEG: Mind your own business.

LISELOTTE [*on the alert*]: Sure, Mama.

FRAU VON WIEG: What's wrong with you? Why are you dawdling around here?

LISELOTTE: Am I dawdling?

FRAU VON WIEG: I forbid you behaving so shamelessly.

LISELOTTE [*laughs*]: Now you don't like my behavior?

FRAU VON WIEG: All of a sudden your behavior is different.

LISELOTTE What kind of behavior is it then?

FRAU VON WIEG: At any rate it is not the behavior of a young lady.

LISELOTTE [*laughs*]: Let's wait and see which kind of behavior Uncle Dietrich likes best.

FRAU VON WIEG [*explodes*]: Now what do you want from Uncle Dietrich?

LISELOTTE: My behavior—or your behavior.

FRAU VON WIEG: Go to your room at once and practice.

LISELOTTE [*simply*]: Not today, Mama.

FRAU VON WIEG: When do you actually get your diploma?

LISELOTTE [*laughs*]: Not today either, Mama. Do you want to receive Uncle Dietrich in that dress?

FRAU VON WIEG [*curtly*]: I don't have any other.

LISELOTTE: Should I lend you one?

FRAU VON WIEG: Leave me alone. [*Explodes.*] I have to be alone now.

LISELOTTE [*slowly*]: Sure, Mama.

[LISELOTTE *exits slowly.*]

[FRAU VON WIEG *falls helplessly onto a chair.*]

[*The stage goes dark.*]

[*Area 6, the kitchen, lights up.*]

[ERNESTINE; MIMI ZERL, *the housemaid, twenty years old.*]

MIMI [*incredulous*]: If you're having a baby, aren't you supposed to have a big belly in front?

ERNESTINE: I don't.

MIMI: You're crazy.

ERNESTINE: Don't laugh.

MIMI: You want to throw the bucket at my head?

ERNESTINE: God help you if you laugh at me again.

MIMI: Like I said, you're crazy.

ERNESTINE: Like you know what's what.

MIMI: Anyway, you don't have a baby.

ERNESTINE: It's eight months now.

MIMI [*hits her on the belly*]: Oh no, it isn't.

ERNESTINE: It's a very little one. Like you know anything about it.

MIMI: Eight months?

ERNESTINE: Here's the doctor's certificate saying I'm pregnant. [*Pulls a paper out of her purse.*]

MIMI: Why do you need a note?

ERNESTINE: I have it in writing. [*Sticks the paper back inside.*] From the day Gustav moved in upstairs. It happened the very first night.

MIMI: Lucky you.

ERNESTINE: That's what I think.

MIMI: What're you going to call it?

ERNESTINE: You'll be the last to know.

MIMI [*laughs*]: I can wait. Hopefully it'll look like him.

ERNESTINE: What do you mean by that? Maybe you fancy him.

MIMI: That Gustav leaves me cold.

ERNESTINE: You with your nose in the air. As if we'd have anything to do with you.

MIMI: I wouldn't put up with the likes of you either.

ERNESTINE: Kiss my ass.

[*The bell rings.*]

[MIMI *exits laughing.*]

[*The stage goes dark.*]

[*Area 5,* FRAU BERLESSEN'*s living room, lights up.*]

[JOSEF, *in hat and overcoat;* MIMI.]

MIMI [*smiles*]: Did the gentleman ring?

JOSEF: It's too stuffy in here.

MIMI: That's why the gentleman visits the master and mistress so seldom.

JOSEF [*laughs*]: If you weren't here, you little snail.

[JOSEF *grabs* MIMI.]

MIMI [*screams*]: I'm ticklish.

JOSEF [*laughs*]: That's a new one.

MIMI: Let me go, will you. What if Herr Alfred caught us.

JOSEF: I've already seen to that.

MIMI: He wants to run away with the mistress. I heard it myself twice.

JOSEF: Pack of imbeciles. Just what did you hear?

MIMI: Only he needs money, he told her.

JOSEF: Yes, money.

MIMI: What did you bring me?

JOSEF: Is today your day off?

MIMI: And I'm going out. At 9:00.

JOSEF: What about your mistress?

MIMI: It's too stuffy around here for me too. The cook is having a baby.

JOSEF: Whose is it?

MIMI: Tunichtgut, the waiter. The mistress knows about it and wants to pay for the midwife.

JOSEF: As if they still had the money.

MIMI [*laughs*]: Her honorable son wouldn't let her.

JOSEF [*laughs*]: Thank God. So—nine, then.

MIMI: You'll stand us a treat, chubby.

JOSEF: Little snail.

[MIMI *screams.*]

[FRANK, *nineteen years old, enters.*]

JOSEF: You—

[MIMI *exits.*]

JOSEF: Look after your friend in the furnished room.

FRANK: What the crap business is it of yours?

JOSEF [*laughs*]: I am definitely *persona non grata* around here.

[JOSEF *exits.*]

[FRANK *goes into* ALFRED's *room.*]

[*Area 4,* ALFRED's *room, lights up.*]

[ALFRED, *motionless in a chair.*]

FRANK [*sits beside him; after a pause*]: Has Ottfried been here?

ALFRED: No.

[*Pause.*]

FRANK: Penny for your thoughts?

ALFRED [*looks at* FRANK]: We keep secrets from one another.

[FRANK *is silent.*]

ALFRED: We are not the same any more.

FRANK: If you say so.

ALFRED: You don't care for me anymore.

FRANK: Yes, I do, Alfred.

ALFRED: I know it well enough. What's going on with you?

FRANK: What's going on with you?

ALFRED: Then we'd better not talk.

FRANK: If you say so.

ALFRED: I thought you'd have noticed what's been going on.

FRANK: Going on with whom?

ALFRED: I only meant.

FRANK: Then say it.

ALFRED [*looks at him*]: You're barely listening. Every man lives for himself alone.

FRANK: Maybe something's going on with me too.

ALFRED: I'm listening.

FRANK [*laughs maliciously*]: A lot of good that'll do.

ALFRED: You've changed a lot.

FRANK: You said that already.

ALFRED: It wouldn't mean a thing to you—even if I took my life.

FRANK [*perks up*]: You want to take your life?

ALFRED: As if you care.

FRANK: Why do you want to take your life?

ALFRED: Maybe something doesn't suit me anymore.

FRANK: Have you still got my mother on the brain?

ALFRED: The phrases you use.

FRANK: That's only normal.

ALFRED: What's normal?

FRANK: You've got a virile nature, so you desire the first good-looking woman you come across.

ALFRED: You.

FRANK: That's perfectly natural. It's up to her whether she goes along or not.

ALFRED: She's right when she says you hate her.

FRANK [*laughs*]: I don't hate her. She's a stranger to me.

ALFRED: Is that normal too?

FRANK: No, that is quite abnormal.

ALFRED: So you're abnormal?

FRANK: As if you know what's normal.

ALFRED: For the last six months—

FRANK: I have changed. How often are you going to say it? I've even made a discovery.

ALFRED: What kind of discovery?

FRANK: Plenty of people know about it already. Only my best friend and my dear mama haven't a clue.

ALFRED: Haven't a clue about what?

FRANK: Because they're so self-involved.

ALFRED: Are you going to be rude?

FRANK: Get stuffed.

ALFRED: Do you think there's the least little thing between her and me?

FRANK: If you don't give it up, it's bound to happen. No woman can withstand a persistent young man for long. And certainly not a woman who's had nothing from life.

ALFRED: All the more reason to respect her.

FRANK: That's the best way to begin. You certainly won't take your life. Me first.

ALFRED: Why you?

FRANK [*sardonic*]: Guess.

ALFRED [*excited*]: You're in love too?

FRANK: If you can call it love.

ALFRED: Madly?

FRANK: Madly, I suppose.

ALFRED: With whom?

FRANK: Guess.

ALFRED: You know *my* secret.

FRANK: Guess.

ALFRED: If you don't want to tell me, then keep it to yourself.

FRANK: That won't do me any good.

ALFRED: You always talk in riddles.

FRANK: Other people know it besides my brother Josef.

ALFRED: Josef?

FRANK: He even told me to look after you.

ALFRED: If I do take my life, I'll shoot him first.

[FRANK *laughs.*]

ALFRED: That monster is the cause of your family's misfortunes.

FRANK: If you love a woman, don't bother about her family—you still haven't guessed.

ALFRED: What am I supposed to guess?

FRANK: You haven't been paying attention.

ALFRED: Speak clearly or keep still.

FRANK: Some things can't be said clearly.

ALFRED: Only in a twisted mind.

FRANK: Then I must be twisted. That's a new one.

ALFRED: I didn't say you were twisted.

FRANK: Never mind.

ALFRED [*more heatedly*]: Just what's wrong with you?

FRANK: Never mind. Every man lives for himself alone.

ALFRED: That's not what I meant.

FRANK [*looks at him*]: When we were boys, we often played doctor. Do you remember?

ALFRED: Doctor?

FRANK: You were the patient and I was the doctor.

ALFRED: What are you getting at?

FRANK: Nothing. We were only playing.

ALFRED: I remember that we played world war.

FRANK: That too. Then you were always the wounded Frenchman, and I had to bind your wounds. So we were playing doctor there too. I touched your whole body to see where you were hurt.

ALFRED: I don't understand.

FRANK: You've forgotten. That's quite normal.

ALFRED: And what's the point of our boyhood games?

FRANK: That's the discovery I made.

ALFRED: Playing doctor? A medical discovery?

FRANK [*laughs*]: A medical discovery.

ALFRED: How long are you going to play me for a fool?

FRANK [*suddenly*]: What would you say if we died together?

ALFRED [*startled*]: I will never understand you.

FRANK [*passionately*]: Alfred, in the name of our long friendship. We grew up together, let us die together.

ALFRED [*uneasy*]: Now I'm starting to get scared.

FRANK: Blow my brains out, so that finally, finally I'll be at peace. I'll see to the revolver.

ALFRED: Frank.

FRANK: I beseech you.

ALFRED: I'd better call a doctor.

FRANK [*leaps up*]: I cannot stand it any longer. I want to put an end to it all.

ALFRED [*follows him*]: Say what you have to say at last.

[FRANK *falls into* ALFRED's *arms and starts to sob.*]

ALFRED [*quietly*]: Say it.

FRANK [*quietly*]: Can't you understand?

ALFRED [*quietly*]: I can't understand a word. Have you stolen something? Have you embezzled money?

FRANK: If I tell you—will you shoot me?

ALFRED: I don't know yet.

FRANK: Promise me, Alfred.

ALFRED: You're not in your right mind.

FRANK: Promise me, Alfred.

ALFRED: [*holds* FRANK *tight*]: Your whole body is trembling.

FRANK: Promise me, Alfred.

ALFRED: I won't be a murderer.

FRANK: You will shoot yourself too.

ALFRED: I haven't decided yet whether I'll take my life.

FRANK: You still want to think it over.

ALFRED: I am not yet fully convinced.

FRANK [*pulls free, smiling*]: You see how far we are from one another?

ALFRED: All I said was—

FRANK: Very far, even when we look into one another's eyes.

ALFRED: —I still want to think it over.

FRANK [*in control again*]: When things get serious, you back out.

ALFRED: There's good reason to think over a decision like that.

FRANK: It would be crazy to do it on account of a woman, when there are so many women in the world.

ALFRED: Remarks like that are driving us even farther apart.

FRANK: As if I cared.

ALFRED: Keep your twisted secret—

FRANK [*laughs*]: Then I am twisted.

ALFRED: —and stop trying to pry into my affairs.

FRANK: Idiot.

ALFRED: Now you sound like your brother.

FRANK: Will you soon hate me as you do him?

[ALFRED *is silent.*]

FRANK: Then I still expect you to shoot me.

ALFRED [*maliciously*]: I won't do you the pleasure.

FRANK [*looks at him, calmly*]: Should I slap your face?

ALFRED [*calmly*]: Try it.

FRANK: Once again: idiot.

ALFRED: You're dead to me.

[*Area 5,* FRAU BERLESSEN's *living room, lights up.*]

[OTTFRIED *walks through the space to the door to* ALFRED's *room, which he opens.*]

FRANK: Ottfried, at last,!

[FRANK *goes with* OTTFRIED *into the living room.*]

OTTFRIED: Good evening, Herr Fischau.

ALFRED [*curtly*]: Good evening.

[ALFRED *slams the door behind* OTTFRIED.]

[*Area 4 goes dark.*]

FRANK [*uneasy*]: I couldn't wait for you any longer.

OTTFRIED: Shall we sit down?

FRANK: Spit it out.

OTTFRIED: If we don't consider this calmly, we will do something stupid.

FRANK: Easy for you to be calm.

OTTFRIED: And you're acting as if you were going to be executed. It's just a simple matter of a subpoena to be a witness.

FRANK: Ottfried.

OTTFRIED [*quietly*]: Unfortunately, there's no way out of it.

FRANK: What about the money?

OTTFRIED: What money?

FRANK: I gave the hairdresser a hundred and eighty marks so that Schimmelweis wouldn't mention me.

OTTFRIED: You mean the hundred and twenty marks from before?

FRANK: No. Three days ago, Tuesday, he got a hundred and eighty marks because Schimmelweis declared he'd have me called as a witness otherwise. The gold watch, the books, the onyx cuff links—they're all gone.

OTTFRIED: I'd keep an eye on that hairdresser. Who knows how much he kept for himself.

FRANK: I can't take it to him myself.

OTTFRIED: With blackmailers you never know the right thing to do.

FRANK: I'll take my life.

OTTFRIED: Of course that would be the most painless solution.

FRANK: I don't know any more what I should do.

OTTFRIED: Think it over.

FRANK: I rack my brains. I can't sleep any more. The last ten days. I'm afraid I'm going insane.

OTTFRIED: The main thing—the witness box is not the prisoner's dock.

FRANK: That'll be the next step. There'll be no end to it.

OTTFRIED: Just deny the whole business

FRANK: But I was seen in the bathing cabin with Oskar.

OTTFRIED: You weren't being very cautious.

FRANK: That Schimmelweis knows all the details.

OTTFRIED: Perhaps Oskar himself prattled a bit?

FRANK: You!

OTTFRIED [*laughs*]: I don't mean to tease you.

FRANK: He is the only thing that keeps me going.

OTTFRIED: Nevertheless, you now have to avoid him.

FRANK: Better a bullet.

OTTFRIED: At least until the subpoena.

FRANK: I can hardly wait an hour to be together with him.

OTTFRIED: In any case, you've been warned. [*Casually.*] Could you let me have five hundred marks?

FRANK: Impossible.

OTTFRIED: Then let it slide.

FRANK: But I'm going to go to prison.

OTTFRIED: That depends on your testimony.

FRANK: What are the five hundred marks for?

OTTFRIED: A great big gag to shove in Schimmelweis's mouth.

FRANK: You think so?

OTTFRIED: Then he'll definitely keep it shut.

FRANK: But he's had me called as a witness.

OTTFRIED: His lawyer came up with that.

FRANK: How can I raise five hundred marks?

OTTFRIED: It would be a good thing.

FRANK: Could you borrow it somehow?

OTTFRIED [*laughs*]: I've had to tell my mother fibs about my studies for two hours to pry ten marks loose from her. And I don't get them till tomorrow.

FRANK: That's a pity.

OTTFRIED: What's worse, I'm afraid that Professor Hahn will stop working.

FRANK: Who's Professor Hahn?

OTTFRIED: A mythical crammer, whose name I drop whenever I need money.

FRANK: What money?

OTTFRIED: Haven't you been listening?

FRANK: What money? Don't torture me.

OTTFRIED: Ten marks—calm down.

FRANK: What good are ten marks?

OTTFRIED: That's what I've been saying.

FRANK: What if I report the fellow myself?

OTTFRIED: Then you're admitting to the crime.

FRANK: But it isn't a crime. It's a love like any other.

OTTFRIED [*laughs.*] So I'm told.

FRANK: Will they call you as a witness too?

OTTFRIED: He didn't try to blackmail me. Since it's against the law, I don't let him see a thing.

FRANK: That law is itself a crime.

OTTFRIED: Did you leave a letter to Oskar at the sports club?

FRANK: I haven't seen him in four days.

OTTFRIED: A very explicit letter.

FRANK: How do you know that?

OTTFRIED: There's been talk. How could you let it lie around?

FRANK: While I was writing, I suddenly saw Oskar walking across the lawn. So I ran to him.

OTTFRIED: Be sure and get hold of the letter. The letter is dangerous.

FRANK: You think so?

OTTFRIED: I never write letters.

FRANK: Why are you making that face?

OTTFRIED: In your passion you forget everything and behave like a child. Letters like that have cost a great many men their necks.

FRANK: You think so?

OTTFRIED: I would like to help you out.

FRANK [*with intense anxiety*]: You think so? That would be the last straw.

OTTFRIED: Just don't lose your head.

FRANK [*calmly*]: I'm no match for this witch hunt. If I don't have the letter back in my hands before the Schimmelweis trial, I'll end it all.

OTTFRIED: First, let me poke around a bit at the sports club. Maybe the swimming instructor or the librarian knows something.

FRANK: I'm not on the best of terms with the librarian.

OTTFRIED: That's stupid. [*Casually.*] Get your hands on a thousand marks.

FRANK: What for?

OTTFRIED: A thousand.

FRANK [*laughs*]: And five hundred for Schimmelweis, so fifteen hundred. Fifteen hundred marks.

OTTFRIED: No silly laughs. How do you know how much you might have to pay for the letter.

FRANK: Where am I going to get fifteen hundred marks? You're crazy. You take me for a millionaire?

OTTFRIED: You're screaming at me as if I wanted the money for myself.

FRANK: There are limits to everything.

OTTFRIED [*threatening*]: You want to reproach me with that?

FRANK: I'm only saying that there are limits to everything.

OTTFRIED: Then sort it out by yourself.

[OTTFRIED *makes to go*.]

FRANK: I'm not a millionaire, my dear.

OTTFRIED: This is ridiculous. You're exploiting my friendship.

FRANK [*astonished*]: When did I ever exploit your friendship?

OTTFRIED: Six months ago I revealed to you your true nature. I introduced you to the sports club. You thanked me for it all. I was near to starting something with you, when you saw Oskar at the sports club, and you were done for.

FRANK: Are you angry with me?

OTTFRIED: I am merely stating facts. I remained your good friend. Whenever one of us had to pay for something, I did it.

FRANK: I don't understand.

OTTFRIED: When the two of us or a threesome with Oskar went out, I always paid the check. And who paid for the automobile excursions, and once didn't I even settle your tailor's bill?

FRANK: I paid you back for the tailor later on.

OTTFRIED: What about the hotels? While you were having a good time, I was living on air.

FRANK: Ottfried!

OTTFRIED: So it tends to annoy me when you indulge in innuendo.

FRANK: What innuendo?

OTTFRIED: Drop it.

FRANK: What innuendo?

OTTFRIED: Have I ever asked you for anything? What do I care about your millions.

FRANK: I have never accused you of it.

OTTFRIED: Drop it. Have you grasped the situation?

FRANK: Fully.

OTTFRIED: That's all I want. Once you know your enemy, you know how to defend yourself.

FRANK: Thank you kindly.

OTTFRIED: Good-bye.

FRANK: Are you angry with me?

OTTFRIED: Don't be ridiculous. Watch out for yourself.

FRANK [*quietly*]: I'll get the fifteen hundred marks.

OTTFRIED: Good-bye.

FRANK: Why are you in such a hurry?

OTTFRIED: I don't want to have anything more to do with the matter.

FRANK: You're leaving me in the lurch?

OTTFRIED: Then you need me?

FRANK: Ottfried, don't leave me alone now.

OTTFRIED: If only I weren't so good to you!

FRANK: I'll pawn the silverware. In this house nobody knows when something goes missing.

OTTFRIED: Your mother doesn't notice either?

FRANK: She has other things to worry about.

OTTFRIED: You have to be extremely careful. But I won't get involved.

FRANK: Ever since Josef moved out, everything's gone to hell around here.

OTTFRIED: Anyway you'd better hurry up—if you want it to work.

FRANK: You can have it tomorrow.

OTTFRIED: I? What's it got to do with me?

FRANK [*anxious*]: Aren't you going to retrieve the letter for me?

OTTFRIED: I can only try to find out who has it. Then I'll arrange a meeting in Café Wolff. You will make an apology that you are prevented from showing up and punctually send the money.

FRANK: By whom?

OTTFRIED [*casually*]: Whomever you like—maybe the hairdresser.

[FRANK *sighs*.]

OTTFRIED: You confided in him once. Give him a couple of marks.

FRANK [*laughs*]: That's just what I need.

OTTFRIED: Anyway, you've already tested his discretion. But it's up to you. The main thing—no meetings with Oskar.

FRANK: We're meeting at 8:30.

OTTFRIED: You are an incorrigible sinner.

FRANK [*pulls a revolver out of his pocket*]: You know what this is.

OTTFRIED [*coldly*]: I have no understanding of such things.

FRANK: Ottfried?

OTTFRIED: Yes.

FRANK [*pauses*]: You have no understanding of such things.

OTTFRIED: No. Just a couple of months ago you were brimming over with life. I never would have fallen for you otherwise. You're unrecognizable.

FRANK: Alfred says so too.

OTTFRIED: Good-bye—

FRANK: Ottfried—

OTTFRIED: Yes?

FRANK [*pauses*]: Take this with you. [*Gives* OTTFRIED *the revolver.*] Are you satisfied now? Sometimes I really think that things can't go on.

OTTFRIED: At closer inspection, things always go on.

[*The stage goes dark.*]

[*Area 7, backroom of* KARLA KUDELKA*'s bar, lights up.*]

[TUNICHTGUT; *the* KUDELKA *woman.*]

TUNICHTGUT [*putting on his jacket*]: I'd better climb out the window.

KUDELKA [*laughs*]: If you want to.

TUNICHTGUT: She's out running errands, the missus.

KUDELKA [*remakes the bed*]: If she catches you, will she beat your brains out?

TUNICHTGUT: I don't like quarrels. Madame is inclined to be jealous.

KUDELKA: That I can understand.

TUNICHTGUT [*smartly*]: Is that supposed to be an unsolicited testimonial?

KUDELKA [*laughs*]: In every way. You know what's what. Give me another kiss. You're sensational.

TUNICHTGUT: Experience does it.

KUDELKA: When you going to get a job?

TUNICHTGUT: The Lord will provide.

KUDELKA: Women, you mean.

TUNICHTGUT [*laughs*]: I'm no shrinking violet.

KUDELKA: Neither am I.

TUNICHTGUT: You're supposed to have a hidden treasure. The taxi driver Weis and I were planning to break into your place.

KUDELKA: You don't have to. But I expect that of him.

TUNICHTGUT: Where have you tucked away your famous treasure?

[KUDELKA *goes offstage, into the front of the bar.* TUNICHTGUT *follows* KUDELKA *as far as the door.* KUDELKA *gives* TUNICHTGUT *money. They both laugh.*]

TUNICHTGUT: That's what I call generous.

KUDELKA [*offstage*]: Well, I've had something from you in return.

[*They both laugh.*]

[*The* KUDELKA *woman suddenly runs back in.*]

KUDELKA: That Puschek woman is coming.

[TUNICHTGUT *goes out the window.*]

[ERNESTINE *enters.*]

ERNESTINE: Has Gustav just been here?

KUDELKA: Who exactly do you mean?

ERNESTINE: So you're lying.

KUDELKA: I don't know any Gustav.

ERNESTINE: The waiter Tunichtgut.

KUDELKA: Haven't seen him.

ERNESTINE: You aren't that blind.

KUDELKA: He was a waiter in my bar?

ERNESTINE: You never had a waiter.

KUDELKA: So just what do you want?

ERNESTINE: You look after everything in the bar yourself. And I do mean everything.

KUDELKA: That's none of your business.

ERNESTINE: Even the entertainment.

KUDELKA: Look here, you'd better clear out.

ERNESTINE: The police should have a look around.

KUDELKA: There's the door.

ERNESTINE: Maybe you water down the booze yourself.

KUDELKA You must be drunk.

ERNESTINE: But I won't let anybody fool with my man.

KUDELKA: You'd better sew him into your skirts.

ERNESTINE: I don't need your advice. I don't want it to end in the reformatory.

KUDELKA: Who's going to the reformatory?

ERNESTINE: Maybe you.

KUDELKA: Say that again.

ERNESTINE: Because you're peddling flesh without a license.

KUDELKA [*pouncing on* ERNESTINE]: Get out, you cow.

ERNESTINE: Then let Gustav alone. He's meat for your betters.

[ERNESTINE *is about to go.*]

KUDELKA: I don't even know him.

ERNESTINE [*eyeing* KUDELKA]: You don't know him?

KUDELKA: Never laid eyes on him.

ERNESTINE: He was never with you?

KUDELKA: Never.

ERNESTINE: Now you're lying.

KUDELKA: Are you starting that again?

ERNESTINE: Yesterday on the stairs, didn't he tip his hat to you?

KUDELKA: Lots of people tip their hats to me.

ERNESTINE: I can just imagine. And he never got a bottle of beer?

KUDELKA: Two, for all I care.

ERNESTINE: So he was here twice?

KUDELKA: I've had just about enough of this.

ERNESTINE: Well, I haven't. So he's lying too.

KUDELKA: Take it up with him.

ERNESTINE: He was here twice. He told me he was here only once.

KUDELKA: I've got to go back to the bar.

ERNESTINE: Stay here and answer me.

KUDELKA: I'm not crazy.

ERNESTINE: There's nobody in the bar. Three times?

KUDELKA: Ten times, you bitch.

[KUDELKA *tears herself away.* ERNESTINE *pounces on* KUDELKA *from behind and pulls her to the floor.*]

ERNESTINE: Now tell the truth.

KUDELKA: Let go, or I'll scream.

ERNESTINE, Go on, scream. How often has he been with you?

KUDELKA [*A glance; fearful*]: Are you going to strangle me?

ERNESTINE: Tell the truth, and I'll let you go.

KUDELKA [*after a pause*]: Never.

ERNESTINE [*immediately lets* KUDELKA *go*]: Never? Say it again.

KUDELKA: Never.

ERNESTINE [*quietly*]: He did swear it on the life of his child.

KUDELKA: Well, then.

ERNESTINE: Never, you said?

KUDELKA: Never.

ERNESTINE: Then I beg your pardon.

KUDELKA: You've got a heavy hand.

ERNESTINE: That's why I'm apologizing.

KUDELKA: When you're going to have a baby any minute.

ERNESTINE: I lost my wits.

KUDELKA: You shouldn't get so overwrought, when you're that far gone with a baby.

ERNESTINE [*strokes* KUDELKA's *arm*]: Thank you.

KUDELKA: Now get out of here.

ERNESTINE: When a woman wants to hold on to something, it's always a matter of life and death.

KUDELKA: Jealousy won't help you hold on to him.

ERNESTINE: Because today he parted his hair just so.

KUDELKA: Get out of here.

ERNESTINE: A woman really has to look out for herself. A woman can chew herself to bits with her thoughts.

KUDELKA: Why do you keep looking around?

ERNESTINE: I'll go now. He certainly is the nicest guy.

KUDELKA: In that case, I'd be happy and keep my mouth shut.

ERNESTINE: I know him through and through. He wouldn't hurt a fly. But he has lots of needs. [*Intimately.*] Sometimes it goes on all night long.

KUDELKA: Is that so.

ERNESTINE: He never has enough.

KUDELKA: Keep it to yourself.

ERNESTINE [*laughs*]: He is a real man, always wild, you should see him sometimes.

KUDELKA [*laughs*]: Now you're being silly.

ERNESTINE [*laughs*]: Really attractive, I tell you.

KUDELKA [*laughs*]: A sensation. He's sure gone to your head.

ERNESTINE: No wonder a woman gets a baby right away. He's enough for ten women.

KUDELKA [*pushing* ERNESTINE *to the door*]: What're you going to call it?

ERNESTINE: Theobald, if it's a boy.

KUDELKA: Theobald.

ERNESTINE: Theobald sounds good.

KUDELKA: Very good.

ERNESTINE [*finally seeing what she's looking for, running to the night table*]: And whose is the watch?

KUDELKA [*panicked*]: What watch?

ERNESTINE: This one here, with the gold chain?

KUDELKA: How did that watch get there?

[KUDELKA *suddenly tries to escape.* ERNESTINE *blocks the exit.*]

ERNESTINE: Take a good look at it.

KUDELKA: I've had enough of this.

ERNESTINE: You've had enough? It happens to be mine.

KUDELKA: For all I know, it's the king of China's.

ERNESTINE: I gave it to him as a gift. And he got the gramophone from me too. Everything he's got, he got from me.

KUDELKA: Then maybe he's had enough of you.

ERNESTINE: Please say that again.

KUDELKA: I'm younger than you and not the missus.

ERNESTINE: You are younger. But I'll fix you yet, you slut. Soon you'll be older than I am, soon you'll be real old, so old that you'll be dead.

KUDELKA [*tries to scream*]: Murder! Murder!

ERNESTINE [*grasps* KUDELKA *by the throat*]: Go on and scream. She worms it all out of me, when she knows it already.

KUDELKA [*hoarsely*]: I'm choking.

ERNESTINE: A sensation, you slut. And the beefsteak on the table?

KUDELKA: Let go.

ERNESTINE: Was he here?

KUDELKA: Let go.

ERNESTINE: Was he here or not?

KUDELKA: Yes.

ERNESTINE: So he likes your cooking better than mine.

KUDELKA: I don't know.

ERNESTINE: The cooking too. One-stop shopping.

KUDELKA: Help!

[KUDELKA *tries to get away*; ERNESTINE *comes after her*.]

ERNESTINE: The cooking too. And I'm a poor cow—

KUDELKA [*running*]: They should lock you in a madhouse.

ERNESTINE [*after her*]: —who wanted to give him a kid too.

[KUDELKA *escapes into the front of the bar*. ERNESTINE *follows her. Both are offstage*.]

KUDELKA: Help!

[KUDELKA *screams; chairs fall over*. ERNESTINE *comes back, sets herself to rights before the mirror and exits*.]

[*The area goes dark*.]

[*Area 1*, FRAU VON WIEG's *room, lights up*.]

[FRAU VON WIEG; DIETRICH VON WIEG, *her brother-in-law*.]

DIETRICH: You don't expect me to be satisfied with such explanations.

FRAU VON WIEG: What else could I do?

DIETRICH: The public prosecutor will fill you in.

FRAU VON WIEG [*hushed*]: Dietrich.

DIETRICH: Sentimentality doesn't work on me.

FRAU VON WIEG: I only want to remind you that they are the children of your late brother.

DIETRICH: The jewelry was worth thirty thousand marks. Have you paid out thirty thousand marks for the children's education over three years?

FRAU VON WIEG: Whenever the items had to be sold, they were suddenly worth nothing.

DIETRICH [*rises*]: Three years ago I turned the jewelry over to you for safekeeping, since I had to go to South America. I give you three days in which to turn it over to me again.

FRAU VON WIEG: The court will understand the feelings of a mother, who sacrificed everything for her children's education. You have no children, no wife. Or did you get married over there?

DIETRICH: I am not crazy.

FRAU VON WIEG: You've become very wealthy over there. Cancel the debt.

DIETRICH: And what have your children achieved?

FRAU VON WIEG [*proud*]: Ottfried will be a doctor of art history in two years. Liselotte is getting a diploma as a state-certified piano teacher.

DIETRICH: Nowadays any rational education would protect the children from careers in the arts as from the plague.

FRAU VON WIEG: It's a matter of fundamentals.

DIETRICH: You're living on Mars.

[DIETRICH *exits*.]

[FRAU VON WIEG *remains immobile*.]

[*The stage goes dark*.]

[*Area 6, the kitchen, lights up*.]

[TUNICHTGUT; MIMI.]

TUNICHTGUT [*slickly*]: I'm a perfect gentleman, my good woman.

MIMI [*laughs*]: I like you a lot.

TUNICHTGUT: I wouldn't mind taking you on a tour of Luna Park.

MIMI: The Puschek woman would kill us both dead.

TUNICHTGUT: First she has to catch us.

MIMI: Are you that clever?

TUNICHTGUT: The young lady may leave it to me.

MIMI: You must have a lot of experience?

TUNICHTGUT: I know my way around. The closer you stay to home, the safer you are.

MIMI: You are foxy.

TUNICHTGUT: And the danger increases the pleasure. Experience in love is the best school for life. Have you read Stendhal?

MIMI: Is that a book?

TUNICHTGUT: A traveler left it in his hotel room. I make so bold as to lend you my copy, and recommend that you pay particular attention to the passages underlined in red.

MIMI: Did you give it to the Puschek woman to read?

TUNICHTGUT: No. She belongs to the breed of primitive creatures. Intellectual seeds don't sprout in that soil.

MIMI: Are you well educated?

TUNICHTGUT: I wouldn't care to deny it. A waiter must, above all, know human nature. The facial expression, the hand gestures, the gait are enough for me to predict what a guest will order. From the tip—not the amount, but the way it's given—I can tell you almost the exact sum of money the hotel guest has in the bank.

MIMI: Well, I'll be darned, Herr Tunichtgut.

TUNICHTGUT: If the young lady will trust me completely, she will have no reason to regret it.

MIMI: The main thing is I want to get far away from here. Will you help me?

TUNICHTGUT: I am a perfect gentleman, my good woman. Your gleaming teeth could easily rob me of my reason. I put a lot of stock in teeth.

MIMI: I've got all thirty-two.

TUNICHTGUT: The young lady has never been to a dentist?

MIMI: Not yet.

TUNICHTGUT: May I see for myself?

MIMI [*laughs*]: You've got a nerve.

TUNICHTGUT: Your looks make that only natural. [*Kisses* MIMI.]

MIMI: Not here.

TUNICHTGUT: A jealous woman always on the prowl never sees a thing.

MIMI: Is that in the book?

[ERNESTINE *enters.*]

ERNESTINE [*calmly*]: The shops were crowded.

MIMI: Herr Tunichtgut has been waiting for you.

ERNESTINE: You've kept him company, I hope.

MIMI: He came in just a minute ago.

ERNESTINE: You weren't upstairs in your room.

TUNICHTGUT: No.

ERNESTINE [*laughs*]: Then where were you?

TUNICHTGUT: Out for a breath of fresh air.

ERNESTINE: Air?

TUNICHTGUT: What's funny about that?

ERNESTINE: Not a thing. Do you want something to eat?

TUNICHTGUT: No, thanks.

ERNESTINE: You're not hungry?

TUNICHTGUT: Maybe later.

ERNESTINE: Maybe you've eaten already?

TUNICHTGUT: Why should I have eaten already?

ERNESTINE: Because you're not hungry.

TUNICHTGUT: I will be.

ERNESTINE: I won't insist. [*Puts down the plates.*] Set the table.

TUNICHTGUT: The young lady wants to leave us.

ERNESTINE: Is that so?

MIMI: Three weeks are enough for me.

ERNESTINE: I've been here eight months now.

[ERNESTINE *exits into the dining room.*]

MIMI: You've got your reasons.

TUNICHTGUT: Listen to her, Tinchen.

MIMI: Man and child under one roof.

TUNICHTGUT: You listening?

ERNESTINE [*offstage*]: Of course I'm listening.

TUNICHTGUT [*quietly*]: I told you.

MIMI: Careful.

TUNICHTGUT [*laughs*]: Jealousy makes them deaf.

MIMI: You're crazy. [*Pulls free.*]

[ERNESTINE *comes in again.*]

ERNESTINE [*as though she's noticed nothing*]: Is the coffee service still upstairs?

TUNICHTGUT [*quickly*]: I'll bring it down.

ERNESTINE: Never mind.

[ERNESTINE *hurries out.*]

MIMI [*astonished*]: She didn't notice a thing.

TUNICHTGUT: It's all in Stendhal. Now quick.

[TUNICHTGUT *and* MIMI *embrace tightly.*]
[*The stage goes dark.*]
[*Area 2,* OLGA NAGERLE's *room, lights up.*]
[OLGA *at the typewriter; the student* KUMMERER *is reading.*]

OLGA: But it's falsifying a birth.

KUMMERER: Don't worry about it.

OLGA: We'll be arrested and end up in prison.

KUMMERER: We will be safe. And it's better than an abortion. [*Very affectionately, leans on* OLGA]. So long as our love keeps us together, poverty won't get the better of us.

OLGA [*embraces* KUMMERER]: You. [*Goes on typing.*]

KUMMERER: So long as the birth isn't painful.

OLGA [*quietly*]: In my heart of hearts I'd like to keep it.

KUMMERER [*full of love*]: We put that out of our minds.

OLGA [*quietly*]: Let me keep it.

KUMMERER: Don't you think that it's always on my mind?

OLGA: Let me keep it.

KUMMERER: While we ourselves are starving?

OLGA: But we're living all the same.

KUMMERER: Off the leftovers of people we don't even know. What if the Puschek woman didn't bring you milk, with your weak lungs.

[OLGA *begins to sob.*]

KUMMERER [*strokes* OLGA*'s head*]: This is the best solution. It's a kind of godsend. Our child will be all right with that woman.

OLGA [*quietly*]: Yes.

KUMMERER: Better than with us.

OLGA: If she would only adopt it.

KUMMERER: She has her reasons.

OLGA: So it will be a crime.

KUMMERER: There's no other way out. Let's go on with our work. The article on free will in Kant and Leibnitz is bound to bring me ten marks.

OLGA: Tomorrow morning I'll get the money for the typing. Fourteen marks.

KUMMERER: The main thing is you need a pair of shoes.

OLGA: I'll bring the money straight to the landlord. Otherwise we'll be sitting in the street.

[ERNESTINE *pops in.*]

ERNESTINE: I just wanted to say you can keep your bastard.

KUMMERER [*jumps up*]: Frau Puschek.

[OLGA *falls into* KUMMERER's *arms.*]

[*The area goes dark.*]

[*Area 7, backroom of the bar, lights up.* FIRST POLICE INSPECTOR *from the homicide squad; the hairdresser* KAKS.]

FIRST POLICE INSPECTOR: Did you notice what time it was when you heard the scream?

KAKS: No, Inspector.

FIRST POLICE INSPECTOR: You should have done.

KAKS: You don't think about things like that. Right after the screams, I tried to get into the bar. I found it locked, which struck me as suspicious. I went to get a locksmith. When I saw the Kudelka woman lying dead on the floor, I immediately informed the police.

FIRST POLICE INSPECTOR: Is she lying the way you found her?

KAKS: Absolutely. I know how the police like things to be.

[SECOND POLICE INSPECTOR *comes out of the front of the bar.*]

FIRST POLICE INSPECTOR: Have you found the key to the bar?

SECOND POLICE INSPECTOR: No.

FIRST POLICE INSPECTOR: We'll have to have a thorough search.

SECOND POLICE INSPECTOR: The murderer probably locked it from the outside and took it with him.

FIRST POLICE INSPECTOR: Is your shop next door?

KAKS: Yes, Inspector.

FIRST POLICE INSPECTOR: Keep yourself at our disposal.

[FIRST POLICE INSPECTOR *and* SECOND POLICE INSPECTOR *are about to go into the front of the bar.*]

KAKS [*suddenly*]: There is Herr Tunichtgut's watch.

FIRST POLICE INSPECTOR [*immediately*]: Show us the watch.

KAKS: I recognize the gold chain.

FIRST POLICE INSPECTOR: Who is Herr Tunichtgut?

KAKS: An unemployed waiter who lives on the top floor.

FIRST POLICE INSPECTOR: Unemployed? [*To* SECOND POLICE INSPECTOR.] Take the gentleman to his lodgings.

[*Everyone leaves. Area 7, the backroom of the bar, remains lit.*]

[*Simultaneously, area 4,* ALFRED FISCHAU'*s room, lights up.* ALFRED *is writing, lifts his head dreamily, goes on writing. Area 4 goes dark.*]

[*Simultaneously, area 5,* FRAU BERLESSEN'*s living room, lights up.* FRAU BERLESSEN *and* FRANK *are at dinner.*]

FRANK [*calls*]: Won't you come and eat something, Alfred?

[ALFRED *reluctantly closes his exercise book and goes downstairs.*]

[*Area 5 remains lit.*]

[*Simultaneously, area 3,* GUSTAV TUNICHTGUT'*s room, lights up. The door to* TUNICHGUT'*s room is broken in from outside. The* SECOND POLICE INSPECTOR *and the* THIRD POLICE INSPECTOR *enter along with the hairdresser* KAKS.]

SECOND POLICE INSPECTOR: Gave us the slip.

KAKS: Just what I suspected.

THIRD POLICE INSPECTOR: He won't get far.

[KAKS *makes himself scarce;* SECOND POLICE INSPECTOR *and the* THIRD POLICE INSPECTOR *examine the room. Area 3 remains lit.*]

[*Simultaneously, area 2,* OLGA NAGERLE'*s room, lights up.*]

OLGA [*at the typewriter, can't go on any further, rises*]: My heart's about to burst.

KUMMERER: For heaven's sake.

[KUMMERER *goes to* OLGA's *aid; she faints.*]

KUMMERER: I'll get the doctor.

[KUMMERER *exits. Area 2 remains lit.*]

[*Simultaneously, area 1,* FRAU VON WIEG's *room, lights up.* FRAU VON WIEG *alone, takes out the jewel box, dresses, and then exits. Area 1 remains lit.*]

[*Simultaneously, area 6, the kitchen, lights up.* ERNESTINE *is busy at the sideboard.* TUNICHTGUT *is lounging around.* MIMI *is arranging a tray.*]

ERNESTINE [*to* MIMI]: You can start serving. Ask whether the young masters want beer.

[MIMI *exits. We can see the* BERLESSENS *being served in the living room.*]

ERNESTINE [*to* TUNICHTGUT]: Still no appetite?

TUNICHTGUT: I'll finish this cigarette first.

FRAU BERLESSEN [*to* FRANK *and* ALFRED, *who are sitting beside her at the table*]: What's wrong with the two of you?

[*No one looks anyone else in the face.*]

MIMI: Would the young masters like some beer?

FRAU BERLESSEN: You're not very talkative.

[*Area 7, the backroom of the bar.* FIRST POLICE INSPECTOR *comes back out of the main section of the bar with the* CORONER. *Both sit down.*]

FIRST POLICE INSPECTOR: Well, Doctor?

CORONER: The murder took place about half an hour ago.

FIRST POLICE INSPECTOR: So around 7:00.

CORONER: Death by strangulation.

FIRST POLICE INSPECTOR [*making a note*]: An open-and-shut case, and no loose ends.

[*All the lit areas remain lit.*]

[*Life goes on.*]

[*Curtain.*]

ACT II

Criminal court

Top level

Judges' reading room; courtroom 1; corridor with bench

Middle level

Courtroom 2; courtroom 3

Bottom level

Large assize courtroom

Vertical cross-section through three levels

Top	Judges' reading room	Courtroom 1 (Fischau case)	Corridor with bench
Middle	Courtroom 2 (Schimmelweis case)	Courtroom 3 (Nagerle case)	
Bottom	Large assize courtroom (Tunichgut case)		

[*The corridor is lit;* FRANK *and* OTTFRIED *on the bench.*]

FRANK: If you want to keep silent, please do.

OTTFRIED: Did you know Liselotte's going to marry Uncle Dietrich? That girl impresses even me.

FRANK: What I know is that in half an hour I'll be on trial.

OTTFRIED: Schimmelweis is on trial, not you.

FRANK: I'd rather be on trial than have to attest that Schimmelweis is an honest man.

OTTFRIED [*fondly*]: No one is forcing you to do it.

FRANK: Don't humor me.

OTTFRIED: Why so nervous? You still have half an hour.

FRANK: If only it were over.

OTTFRIED: You never can tell.

FRANK: What do you mean by that?

OTTFRIED: Nothing.

FRANK: You really have no heart.

OTTFRIED: Thank God.

FRANK: After all, my whole future is at stake.

OTTFRIED: You have to pay close attention to the details. They're the only things that can twist the noose round your neck.

FRANK: That's nonsense.

OTTFRIED: Does your mother suspect anything?

FRANK: She's got enough on her hands with Alfred. What will Alfred get?

OTTFRIED: A shyster lawyer will get him off with probation. The case is favorable: break in to the pay office, caught right away, gave back all the money, brilliant testimonials from his employers, and the company declares no harm done. The romance of an incompetent and amorous embezzler will easily dispose the judge to be fatherly. I can guess how the story ends.

FRANK: What story?

OTTFRIED: Alfred and your mother will go to America or Italy. She doesn't know you're testifying today?

FRANK [*suddenly*]: What do they give for perjury?

OTTFRIED: Up to ten years' penal servitude.

FRANK [*laughs*]: Great.

OTTFRIED: "Whoever swears falsely, with full knowledge of such falsity, an oath required of him by the other party, referred back to him by the other party, or imposed on him by the Court shall be punished by confinement in a penitentiary not to exceed ten years." Section 153.

FRANK: How come you know it by heart?

OTTFRIED: A person should know the legal code inside out.

FRANK: Extenuating circumstances?

OTTFRIED: Fully applicable to you. Especially section 157, clause 1.

FRANK: Do you know that one by heart too?

OTTFRIED: "If a witness renders himself guilty of perjury or of false affirmation in lieu of an oath, the punishment to be imposed shall be reduced by between one-half and one-quarter, if (1) telling the truth might have given risen to a prosecution against himself for a major or minor crime, or if (2)"—but that's got nothing to do with you.

FRANK: Go on anyway.

OTTFRIED: You want to hear it?

FRANK: It has a certain charm.

OTTFRIED: Reciting like this gives me a truly orgasmic feeling, like holding a blade to someone's throat. "Or if (2) the false statement was made for the benefit of a person in regard to whom he had the right to refuse to testify, if he was not instructed as to this right."

FRANK: So two to five years' penal servitude.

OTTFRIED: That would be the maximum penalty. You might enjoy the benefits of section 161.

FRANK: What are the benefits of section 161?

OTTFRIED: "In any sentence for perjury, except for the cases specified in sections 157 and 158, loss of civil rights and, in addition, permanent incapacity of the convicted person to be heard under oath as a witness or expert, shall be imposed." So, with the exceptions of sections 157 and 158, and your case falls under them.

FRANK: That's just wonderful.

OTTFRIED: You see that the law has a heart.

FRANK: And if I testify that Schimmelweis is a blackmailer?

OTTFRIED: Then you admit to the facts of the case. "Unnatural fornication, whether between persons of the male sex—"

FRANK: "—or of humans with beasts." I know. I've read it a hundred times.

OTTFRIED: Pay close attention to the difference in punishment: only penal servitude. "A sentence of loss of civil rights may also be passed." That "also" is convenient.

FRANK [*firmly*]: However, I would rather go to prison for perjury than for the other. I'd rather commit a crime than be imprisoned as an innocent man.

OTTFRIED: You're not in prison yet.

FRANK [*looks at* OTTFRIED]: So deny it all?

OTTFRIED: Schimmelweis will keep his mouth shut.

FRANK: And what does the law say about subornation of perjury?

OTTFRIED: Who's suborning you?

FRANK: You, perhaps.

OTTFRIED [*laughs*]: The best way to warn you is by literal quotation of the sections of the penal code. Keep that in mind.

FRANK [*laughs*]: You've covered your behind. You have nothing to fear from me.

OTTFRIED: I have nothing to fear from anybody.

FRANK: That may be why nothing's ever happened to you.

OTTFRIED [*after a pause*]: I envy Liselotte South America.

FRANK: I'm jammed between two sections of the code.

OTTFRIED: Are you starting again? How did she manage to wind Uncle Dietrich round her little finger in three days?

FRANK: I'm racking my brains. This half hour will never come to an end. I won't know the answer until I'm standing before the judge. Then I'll answer off the top of my head.

OTTFRIED: Stop it. Here's a coin. Heads or tails?

FRANK [*laughs*]: Heads or tails?

OTTFRIED: Heads, you testify. Tails, you deny everything from start to finish.

FRANK: So tails, I deny it all?

OTTFRIED: Agreed?

FRANK: Better than thinking about it.

OTTFRIED: Agreed? [*Tosses the coin.*] Tails.

FRANK: Tails. Deny everything—

OTTFRIED: —from start to finish.

FRANK [*exhales*]: At least now I have my instructions.

OTTFRIED: That's that.

[*The scene goes dark.*]

[*Large assize courtroom lights up*; *the case against* TUNICHTGUT *is in full swing.*]

[PRESIDING JUDGE; TUNICHTGUT; ADDITIONAL JUDGES; DEFENSE COUNSEL; PUBLIC PROSECUTOR; *large number of* SPECTATORS.]

PRESIDING JUDGE [*to* TUNICHGUT *in the witness box*]: So now you admit you knew Kudelka kept cash in her room?

TUNICHTGUT: Everybody knew it.

PRESIDING JUDGE: But you told the taxi driver Weis that it was easy to break the lock.

TUNICHTGUT: People say all sorts of things.

PRESIDING JUDGE: Do you deny having asked him to join you?

TUNICHTGUT: I was talking big at the time.

PRESIDING JUDGE: About a break-in?

TUNICHTGUT [*laughs*]: If that's all a man's got to talk about.

PRESIDING JUDGE: Is that all you can produce against the taxi driver Weis's testimony?

TUNICHTGUT: You're just talking big yourself.

PRESIDING JUDGE: I warn you to moderate that tone.

TUNICHTGUT: Everybody talks big. It's in the blood. Where would you be if you didn't talk big?

PRESIDING JUDGE: Are you referring to the Court?

TUNICHTGUT: Aren't your black nightgowns talking big?

PRESIDING JUDGE [*offended*]: Who here is wearing a black nightgown?

TUNICHTGUT: Why, the whole row down there. And the black bonnets.

PRESIDING JUDGE: If you hadn't just come out of a holding cell on remand—

TUNICHTGUT [*ingenuously*]: It's all just an act.

PRESIDING JUDGE: —I would have assumed you were drunk.

TUNICHTGUT: You know perfectly well that I'm not the murderer. It's all just an act.

DEFENSE COUNSEL: The defendant is understandably overwrought.

TUNICHTGUT: I wouldn't let an unholy mess like this make me believe I killed anybody.

PRESIDING JUDGE: This is contempt of court.

TUNICHTGUT: Then fine me for contempt.

PRESIDING JUDGE: We shall reserve the right.

TUNICHTGUT: But I didn't murder anyone.

PRESIDING JUDGE: Your defense had considerably better prospects when you made your confession.

TUNICHTGUT: But I retracted it a long time ago.

PRESIDING JUDGE: Insolence will get you nowhere. Only the confession—

DEFENSE COUNSEL: The defendant has recanted the confession.

TUNICHTGUT: I've been pressured.

PRESIDING JUDGE: I warn you about further charges of contempt.

DEFENSE COUNSEL: The defendant is referring to the police interrogation.

TUNICHTGUT: It went on all night without a break till 7:00 in the morning. I didn't have any cigarettes.

PRESIDING JUDGE: What have cigarettes got to do with it?

TUNICHTGUT: The inspector was sitting across from me, smoking nonstop. It made me feel sick.

PRESIDING JUDGE: You could have told him that you can't abide smoke.

TUNICHTGUT: Just the opposite. I'm a chain smoker. A full packet lay on the table.

PRESIDING JUDGE: A full cigarette packet lying on the table is no reason to admit to a murder you haven't committed.

TUNICHTGUT: I only brought up the cigarettes on account of the confession.

PRESIDING JUDGE: Do you suppose for a moment that we believe you?

DEFENSE COUNSEL: When did you make the confession?

TUNICHTGUT: 5:00 in the morning. After six hours of questioning.

PRESIDING JUDGE: Did the inspector tell you, by any chance, you could smoke if you made a confession?

TUNICHTGUT: He winked.

PRESIDING JUDGE: I don't understand.

TUNICHTGUT: He didn't say it, but he winked. He kept his mouth shut and pushed the packet over to me. Of course I couldn't hold out any more and grabbed it. Then he laughed and winked.

PRESIDING JUDGE: What about the confession?

TUNICHTGUT: I wanted to seem grateful.

PRESIDING JUDGE: For a cigarette?

TUNICHTGUT: He'd already had enough aggravation from me.

PRESIDING JUDGE: And did you do him that favor?

TUNICHTGUT: Sure. Nothing'll come of this, I thought. You haven't done anything. He also had a bottle of wine brought in.

PRESIDING JUDGE: What fairy tales are you spinning?

DEFENSE COUNSEL: Did you drink?

TUNICHTGUT: No. I don't drink wine.

PRESIDING JUDGE: You were fully in possession of your faculties when you made the confession?

TUNICHTGUT: Waiters hardly ever drink wine.

PRESIDING JUDGE: Your confession is, moreover, eight pages long and includes all the details of the murder.

TUNICHTGUT: The more I made up, the more cigarettes I got.

PRESIDING JUDGE: Stop these fairy tales about cigarettes. Will you deny that in her last moments the Kudelka woman whispered your name?

TUNICHTGUT: The inspector told me Kudelka wasn't dead yet when they found her. She might have said my name.

PRESIDING JUDGE: Was that possible?

TUNICHTGUT: Everything's possible.

DEFENSE COUNSEL: This mysterious last word is an unverified statement meant to entrap the defendant.

PRESIDING JUDGE: Be that as it may, there is a confession.

TUNICHTGUT: Well, I was with Kudelka that night.

PRESIDING JUDGE: Directly before the murder. Why did you climb out of the window?

[TUNICHTGUT *keeps silent.*]

PRESIDING JUDGE: At least the building custodian claims to have seen you. Did you climb out?

TUNICHTGUT: Yes.

PRESIDING JUDGE: Why did you deny at first to have been in Kudel-ka's room that day?

PUBLIC PROSECUTOR: The record shows that the defendant at first denied even knowing Kudelka.

PRESIDING JUDGE: Is that true?

[TUNICHTGUT *keeps silent.*]

PRESIDING JUDGE: You are stated to have asked at the first inter-rogation, "Who's she?" It was only when you were first shown the watch—

TUNICHTGUT: I was afraid of my girlfriend.

PRESIDING JUDGE: Which one? You had at that time five lovers simultaneously.

TUNICHTGUT: Any self-respecting man would. I was always a per-fect gentleman.

[*Hilarity among the* SPECTATORS.]

PRESIDING JUDGE: You haven't proved it to the Court. A couple of cigarettes and you retract the confession you had made. And with the explanation that you are a perfect gentleman, you admit to facts you once denied. But the Court will not be led astray.

TUNICHTGUT [*exhausted, to* DEFENSE COUNSEL]: Counselor, I swear it.

DEFENSE COUNSEL: Listen carefully and answer properly.

PRESIDING JUDGE: Only the truth will help you out. For three months you were out of a job. How did you get the hundred marks found in your pocket?

[TUNICHTGUT *keeps silent.*]

PRESIDING JUDGE: The cupboard in which the murdered woman put her savings for safekeeping had been broken open. The money in it lay scattered about, as if someone had been rummaging in it shortly before.

TUNICHTGUT: She had been rummaging in it herself.

PRESIDING JUDGE: In haste? And left the cupboard open?

[TUNICHTGUT *keeps silent.*]

PRESIDING JUDGE: Why were you let go from the hotel?

[TUNICHTGUT *keeps silent.*]

DEFENSE COUNSEL: Tell the truth.

TUNICHTGUT: I was caught in the act.

DEFENSE COUNSEL: Women play a large role in the defendant's life.

PRESIDING JUDGE: How did you manage to live when you were unemployed?

TUNICHTGUT: Fräulein Puschek helped me out.

PRESIDING JUDGE: Did you also have intimate relations with Puschek?

TUNICHTGUT: She has a kid by me.

PRESIDING JUDGE: That has proven to be a hoax.

TUNICHTGUT [*laughs*]: The kid? It must be born by now.

PRESIDING JUDGE: Charges have been lodged against your former lover for attempted falsification of maternity.

TUNICHTGUT: You trying to sweet-talk me out of a baby too? Can you do magic around here?

PRESIDING JUDGE: You were Kudelka's lover. You knew that she kept cash in the cupboard. We have not only the taxi driver

Weis's word for that. You were out of work. On the day of the murder you visited Kudelka. By your own admission you left her around 7:00. The coroner puts the onset of death by strangulation at 7:00 on the dot. What do you have to say to that?

TUNICHTGUT: No kidding, it wasn't me.

PRESIDING JUDGE: You still think this is an act?

TUNICHTGUT [*ingenuously*]: Yes, your honor.

PRESIDING JUDGE: Why would we do such a thing?

TUNICHTGUT: To punish me.

PRESIDING JUDGE: Why should we punish you?

TUNICHTGUT: Because I cheated on Puschek while she was carrying a kid of mine.

PRESIDING JUDGE: You consider the Court to be a reform school?

TUNICHTGUT: Yes.

PRESIDING JUDGE: You are mistaken.

[*Hilarity among the* SPECTATORS.]

DEFENSE COUNSEL: I call the Court's attention to the defendant's statement. It is an admission of remorse.

TUNICHTGUT: From now on I'll be faithful to Ernestine.

PRESIDING JUDGE: Your good intentions come somewhat late.

TUNICHTGUT: Better late than never. I won't do it again.

PRESIDING JUDGE: We're delighted.

TUNICHTGUT [*bows*]: Can I go now?

PUBLIC PROSECUTOR: Man, stop playing the fool.

PRESIDING JUDGE: And how do you explain the business with the key?

TUNICHTGUT [*exhausted*]: I'm done in.

PRESIDING JUDGE: How do you explain that the key to the bar was in your room?

TUNICHTGUT [*beside himself*]: I can't explain it at all.

PRESIDING JUDGE: We shall have to take that on ourselves. At the discovery of the body, the street door to the bar was locked. The police could not find the key downstairs. But it was found upstairs on the table in your room.

TUNICHTGUT: It's a riddle to me.

PRESIDING JUDGE: Perhaps we can solve it for you. The murderer could not commit his crime in the backroom, because Kudelka desperately ran into the bar to call to the street for help. The murderer forestalled her and locked the street door. Kudelka must have tried to take possession of the key. A struggle ensued. The overturned chairs bear witness to that. Does this make sense?

TUNICHTGUT: I suppose so.

PRESIDING JUDGE: Then will you finally confess to the whole affair?

TUNICHTGUT: If the torture stops—yes, I confess.

PRESIDING JUDGE: You met with great resistance, the victim's screams, the chairs falling over—you had to deal with that before you could lay hands on all the money. In one fell swoop you grabbed the handful of banknotes which were later found in your pocket. In your haste you even left the cupboard open and escaped through the window.

TUNICHTGUT: It wasn't me, your honor. By all the saints.

PRESIDING JUDGE: Again it wasn't you? Just now it was?

TUNICHTGUT: They hound a man to death around here.

PRESIDING JUDGE: Was it you or wasn't it?

TUNICHTGUT: Pretty soon I won't know myself.

PUBLIC PROSECUTOR: The defendant had already made a similar evasive confession to the examining magistrate at the third interrogation.

DEFENSE COUNSEL: This in no way constitutes a confession to the examining magistrate. The defendant merely said, "No man can know everything he's done."

PRESIDING JUDGE: What did you mean by that?

TUNICHTGUT: A man can do something and not know it.

PRESIDING JUDGE: Have you ever had that experience?

TUNICHTGUT: No.

PRESIDING JUDGE: So how do you know?

TUNICHTGUT: I can imagine.

DEFENSE COUNSEL: The defendant means that the unrelenting interrogation finally drove him to this state of mind.

TUNICHTGUT: The magistrate kept at me so long I didn't know if I was coming or going.

PRESIDING JUDGE: Did he offer you cigarettes too?

TUNICHTGUT: He took my hand.

PRESIDING JUDGE: And that's why you made these statements?

TUNICHTGUT: I knocked myself out to make him understand.

PRESIDING JUDGE: But you weren't intimidated or ambushed in any case.

TUNICHTGUT: At first he was friendly, then he suddenly got tough. He stared at me so hard I thought, *Maybe he knows better than you do.*

PRESIDING JUDGE: You mean you thought, *I can't pull the wool over his eyes.*

TUNICHTGUT: Your honor can twist my thoughts, too, but I didn't do it.

PRESIDING JUDGE: How could the examining magistrate know better than you that you committed a murder?

TUNICHTGUT: The interrogation knocked me out. I can't be alone for a long time. I can't stand it. I get scared that I'm going crazy.

PRESIDING JUDGE: This is new.

TUNICHTGUT: When the examining magistrate keeps harping on the same thing so long, you end up thinking you're capable of anything.

PRESIDING JUDGE: Including murder.

TUNICHTGUT: What if I had gone crazy?

PRESIDING JUDGE: Are you offering a defense of temporary insanity?

TUNICHTGUT: How do I know if I'm crazy or not?

PRESIDING JUDGE: Now you want to convince us that a man doesn't know if he's crazy or not?

TUNICHTGUT: There are times when a man doesn't know.

PRESIDING JUDGE: And at such a time you strangled Kudelka?

TUNICHTGUT: I didn't strangle her. But when I was sitting for six hours alone in a room with the magistrate, across from me, cold as ice, sure of himself, I start thinking, *Maybe he knows better, and you went crazy.*

PRESIDING JUDGE: Do you have criteria to judge whether you are crazy?

TUNICHTGUT [*exhausted*]: How many times do I have to say it?

PRESIDING JUDGE: It's not our fault that we're having a hard time understanding you. Is all this meant to establish a defense of temporary insanity?

TUNICHTGUT: You can say what you like. It wasn't me.

PRESIDING JUDGE: The mere statement, so often repeated, is of no use to us. There are no grounds to accept a plea of temporary insanity. Were you ever in an insane asylum?

TUNICHTGUT: No. Only two years in the army.

[*Hilarity among the* SPECTATORS.]

PRESIDING JUDGE: "No man can know everything he's done" is a symptom of temporary insanity?

TUNICHTGUT: Yes.

PRESIDING JUDGE: But you admit that you made this remark as a confession?

TUNICHTGUT: So he would finally believe me.

PRESIDING JUDGE: How's that again?

TUNICHTGUT: It was killing me to see he didn't believe a word so long as I spoke the truth. I felt sorry for him.

PRESIDING JUDGE: So he would finally believe you, you ended up lying?

TUNICHTGUT: Yes.

PRESIDING JUDGE: Defendant, you are lying here, too, and yet we don't believe you.

TUNICHTGUT: I'm sorry.

PRESIDING JUDGE: The facts in the case are clear as day—

[*The area goes dark.*]

[*Courtroom 3 lights up. The case against* OLGA NAGERLE *is in full swing.* PRESIDING JUDGE; ADDITIONAL JUDGES; KUMMERER; OLGA NAGERLE; DEFENSE COUNSEL.]

PRESIDING JUDGE [*to* KUMMERER *in the witness box*]: The facts in the case are clear as day. The defendant Olga Nagerle faked a suicide in the most nefarious way, to rid herself of a baby. Where were you when the defendant drowned the child?

KUMMERER: She didn't drown it.

PRESIDING JUDGE: Answer my question.

KUMMERER: She wanted to take her own life along with the child's. She jumped into the water with the baby.

PRESIDING JUDGE: But she immediately pulled herself out and left the child to drown. The watchman has testified to this peculiar suicide attempt. He saw her swim out of the pond. Before he could go to her aid, she was already safely on land.

KUMMERER: What goes on in a person's mind at such a moment is unfathomable.

PRESIDING JUDGE: You mean the moment when she regretted suicide?

KUMMERER: This mindless fear of death, this unreasoning, automatic instinct for self-preservation—

PRESIDING JUDGE: No lecturing here, please.

KUMMERER: —speaks to the whole pitiful nature of life.

PRESIDING JUDGE: First of all, it speaks to the irresponsibility of conceiving a child.

KUMMERER: We didn't conceive a child.

PRESIDING JUDGE: She, as a once pregnant woman, is in no position to deny it.

KUMMERER [*quietly*]: Your honor, conceiving a child is born of the will to have a child.

PRESIDING JUDGE: Preliminary proceedings reveal that the girl had been used by no man before you.

KUMMERER [*barely in control*]: Your honor!

PRESIDING JUDGE: Chastity may plead extenuating circumstances. At the end of the day, you are the guilty party who forced dishonor on this girl and finally murder.

KUMMERER: We are on different planets.

PRESIDING JUDGE: Drop these childish metaphors. Why didn't you marry the defendant?

KUMMERER: We were too poor.

PRESIDING JUDGE: All the more reason you should have taken care not to bring another hungry mouth into the world. The callousness with which certain intellectual circles, so-called highly educated and emancipated, act nowadays is proven by the matter-of-fact way in which the defendant previously considered the advantages of abortion.

OLGA [*screaming*]: Sentence me and be done with it!

PRESIDING JUDGE: Your wish for expiation is only natural.

OLGA: I can't stand any more of this.

KUMMERER [*very upset*]: Your honor—

PRESIDING JUDGE [*sharply*]: Please don't interrupt me.

KUMMERER: You won't let anyone get a word in edgewise.

PRESIDING JUDGE: We are not here to discuss your absurd philosophy of life.

DEFENSE COUNSEL: May I venture to remark that the defendant has by no means agreed with the witness's superfluous interjections.

OLGA: They've done for us.

PRESIDING JUDGE [*sharply*]: Is the defendant referring to the Court? Or does she after all mean her own defense counsel, who with noteworthy industry is attempting by a demonstration of contrition and shame to elicit a reduced sentence?

KUMMERER [*to* OLGA]: Let's give up. Let him do all the talking.

OLGA [*smiles at him*]: I think of nothing but you.

PRESIDING JUDGE: Did you say something?

[OLGA *and* KUMMERER *are both silent.*]

PRESIDING JUDGE: Where were you when the crime was committed?

KUMMERER: At the university.

PRESIDING JUDGE: How did you react when you first heard of it?

KUMMERER: I wanted to take my life.

PRESIDING JUDGE: I think you mean the defendant?

KUMMERER: She wanted to take her life.

PRESIDING JUDGE: All of a sudden it's both of them.

KUMMERER [*calmly*]: We wanted to take our lives.

PRESIDING JUDGE [*bursts out*]: You should have done it—one is tempted to say. Did you know nothing of the defendant's homicidal intentions?

KUMMERER: Take as an answer whatever you like.

PRESIDING JUDGE: I concur with the public prosecutor's motion, to suspend your testimony until after a corresponding investigation of your possible aiding and abetting. The defendant has stated that she would have had an abortion in time, if she had not planned to get rid of the child as soon as it was born. Did you know about this intended abortion?

OLGA: I never said get rid of.

PRESIDING JUDGE: The court declines to adopt your euphemisms or those of its progenitor. We speak good German here.

OLGA [*after a pause*]: A woman wanted to take the baby, and I trusted her as I would myself.

PRESIDING JUDGE: And, as might have been expected, when the crucial moment arrived, the good fairy declined to put someone else's brat in her nest. And on these offhand assurances that the alleged woman made and, if she did make them, never meant seriously—you brought a new citizen into the world.

KUMMERER: This ostensible and superficial motive doesn't matter. In reality we wanted to keep the child.

PRESIDING JUDGE: What do you mean by "keep"?

KUMMERER: A woman cannot bear a child for nine months without helplessly, if silently, loving it.

PRESIDING JUDGE: And then she murdered it—out of helpless, silent love?

OLGA [*firmly*]: Yes.

PRESIDING JUDGE: So you do admit you murdered it?

OLGA: I admit I loved it.

PRESIDING JUDGE: But I asked if you murdered it?

OLGA: It comes to the same thing.

PRESIDING JUDGE: How is that? It's the same thing that you loved it and you murdered it?

OLGA [*exhausted*]: Yes.

PRESIDING JUDGE: At least you have finally given up the farce of suicide. You went into the water with the child not to commit suicide along with the child but to kill the child.

OLGA [*exhausted*]: Yes.

KUMMERER [*beside himself*]: If we wanted to kill the child from the start, we wouldn't have tried everything to struggle along with the child, and we would not have let it grow to be three weeks old.

PRESIDING JUDGE: That makes it only the more reprehensible.

OLGA [*utterly exhausted*]: Let him speak.

PRESIDING JUDGE: Did you say something?

OLGA: It doesn't matter.

PRESIDING JUDGE: Whereas mitigating circumstances can be found for an infanticide immediately executed, such as pain, loss of blood, fear of death owing to the weakened condition of a woman who's just given birth, there is for the murder of a three-week-old child no distinction between infant or adult. Murder is murder. The cruelest deed, committed by creatures incapable and unworthy of living, in order recklessly to avoid a responsibility imposed by fate as atonement for a moment of lust. Does the witness have anything further to say?

OLGA [*firmly*]: No.

PRESIDING JUDGE [*sharply*]: I will not tolerate your incessant objections, which have no point except to prevent the orderly course of the proceedings. I ask the witness—

[*Courtroom 3 goes dark.*]

[*Courtroom 2 lights up. The Schimmelweis case is in progress.* PRESIDING JUDGE; ADDITIONAL JUDGES; FRANK; DEFENSE COUNSEL; PUBLIC PROSECUTOR; OTTFRIED.]

PRESIDING JUDGE [*indulgently, to* FRANK *in the witness box*]: I ask the witness, will you give your testimony under oath?

FRANK [*firmly*]: Yes.

PRESIDING JUDGE: You are entitled to refuse to testify, if you run the risk of self-incrimination.

FRANK [*hesitating*]: Yes.

PRESIDING JUDGE: So you do refuse to testify?

DEFENSE COUNSEL [*quickly*]: The witness has not fully understood the Court.

FRANK: No.

PRESIDING JUDGE: You haven't fully understood?

DEFENSE COUNSEL [*sharply*]: Of course the witness wishes to make a statement.

FRANK: Yes.

PRESIDING JUDGE: Are you clear about the meaning of an oath?

FRANK: Yes.

PRESIDING JUDGE: Have you ever taken an oath in court?

FRANK: No.

PRESIDING JUDGE: Would you like time to think?

FRANK: Yes.

DEFENSE COUNSEL [*sharply*]: I object to this systematic postponement of the cross-examination of this last witness. The witness has unequivocally expressed his wishes.

FRANK: Yes.

DEFENSE COUNSEL: The witness does not need to be browbeaten.

FRANK: No.

DEFENSE COUNSEL: The witness has nothing to hide and wants to speak out at last.

FRANK: I have nothing to hide.

PRESIDING JUDGE: The court does not intend to be dictated to by the defense, when it comes to making clear to a witness the grave meaning of an oath. Does the prosecution stand with the defense?

PUBLIC PROSECUTOR: To make an end of this, yes.

DEFENSE COUNSEL [*very sharply*]: The trial has so far not provided one iota of proof that the accusation of blackmail against Herr Schimmelweis is justified. This last witness will also be able to say nothing but the truth: Immanuel Schimmelweis is an honest man. It seems all the more urgent that my client finally be released from the embarrassing and dishonorable position of a defendant.

PRESIDING JUDGE [*to* FRANK]: What do you have to say to that?

[FRANK *remains silent.*]

PRESIDING JUDGE: A minor in the eyes of the law is someone who is over fourteen but still not eighteen years old. You are over eighteen, so punishable to the fullest extent of the law.

FRANK: Yes.

PRESIDING JUDGE: Are you aware of that?

FRANK: Yes.

DEFENSE COUNSEL: Are these clearly paternal admonitions meant to intimidate the witness? In the interests of my client, who has the right to breathe fresh air at last, I at this time request the Court, most firmly, to begin with the orderly cross-examination of this witness.

[FRANK *looks for* OTTFRIED, *who is smiling ambiguously at him.*]

PRESIDING JUDGE: We shall proceed to your swearing-in.

FRANK [*very hesitant*]: Yes.

PRESIDING JUDGE: Do you wish to take the oath with the invocation to God?

FRANK [*can barely speak*]: Not to God.

PRESIDING JUDGE: Please repeat after me.

[*The oath is administered.*]

PRESIDING JUDGE: Do you know the defendant?

[*Courtroom 2 does dark.*]

[*Large assize courtroom lights up.* TUNICHTGUT'*s case continues.* PRESIDING JUDGE; ADDITIONAL JUDGES; MIMI ZERL, *very elegantly dressed*; DEFENSE COUNSEL; TUNICHTGUT; COURT OFFICER; PUBLIC PROSECUTOR; CLERK OF THE COURT; *large number of* SPECTATORS.]

PRESIDING JUDGE [*to* MIMI, *in the witness box*]: Do you know the defendant?

MIMI: Through the cook. I never believed in the baby from the get-go.

PRESIDING JUDGE: You were employed as a housemaid in the same family?

MIMI: Housemaid is an exaggeration.

PRESIDING JUDGE: Judging by your outward appearance, you have bettered your situation.

MIMI: My inward appearance too. Now I subscribe to a lending library.

PRESIDING JUDGE: And since that time what has been your occupation?

MIMI: I've been looking around.

PRESIDING JUDGE: What do you mean by that?

MIMI [*genteelly*]: I shall ignore that indiscreet question.

PRESIDING JUDGE: You are in court here.

MIMI [*drops the genteel act*]: That's no reason why should I get the needle.

PRESIDING JUDGE: What does that expression mean?

MIMI: I'm not going to let myself be stitched up.

PRESIDING JUDGE: No one is "stitched up" here.

MIMI: What about Herr Tunichtgut?

PRESIDING JUDGE: I will not tolerate such insinuations.

MIMI: On account of he didn't do it. It could just as well be me.

PRESIDING JUDGE: Are you pleading guilty?

MIMI: You'd like that, wouldn't you?

PRESIDING JUDGE: How do you presume to take this tone in your evidence before the Court?

MIMI: I think you're ridiculous, your honor. Hilarious.

PRESIDING JUDGE: You're not in your own home here.

MIMI: Do you have a clue what goes on in my home?

PRESIDING JUDGE: We would rather not know.

MIMI: But when a person knows life and sees a dozen crimes go on around her every day that you couldn't even dream of, how could this chamber of horrors impress her?

PRESIDING JUDGE: We can dispense with this witness's further testimony.

MIMI: Dispense with all the testimony and the whole shebang. I'd simply organize a lottery every six months. Anyone who draws a blank goes to jail. There he has to draw another lot for how long he'll stay there.

PRESIDING JUDGE [*laughs*]: You choose to amuse the Court.

MIMI: You think that with the lottery more innocents will go to jail? You're dreaming.

DEFENSE COUNSEL: How do you know that the defendant is innocent?

PRESIDING JUDGE: Have you had intimate relations with him too?

MIMI: Unfortunately, you were too quick.

PRESIDING JUDGE: What do you mean by that?

MIMI: We were just about to get into it, when you grabbed him for yourself.

PRESIDING JUDGE: Were you together with him on the day of the murder?

MIMI: It was suppertime in the kitchen. The Puschek woman can testify to that too.

PRESIDING JUDGE: It was 7:30. The murder took place around 7. Defendant, I repeat my question. What did you do between 7 and 7:30?

TUNICHTGUT: Went for a breath of fresh air.

PRESIDING JUDGE: Can you elaborate?

MIMI: Who can elaborate how you get a breath of fresh air?

PRESIDING JUDGE: You insist that you went for a walk, that you met no one, that you went into no shops.

TUNICHTGUT: Yes.

PRESIDING JUDGE: You can't prove an alibi that way.

TUNICHTGUT: I don't always have one on me to pull out of my pocket.

MIMI: Don't let them get you down, Gustav.

DEFENSE COUNSEL: What does the witness know about the defendant?

MIMI: He was a perfect gentleman, and there's damn few of 'em. Nowadays all men look like you, such sourpusses. Mummies all down the line.

PRESIDING JUDGE: The witness will be penalized for contempt of court.

MIMI: I would have fallen in love with him. What difference did it make that he chased after other women? Sex has been sacred from before the flood, which is when you and the whole waxworks here were born, gentlemen.

PRESIDING JUDGE: The witness is immediately dismissed.

MIMI: To stir a lady's love, you need more than a cop's billy club, which is all the manhood you've got, gentlemen. [*To the* COURT OFFICER *who escorts her out.*] Please refrain from pinching my arm.

[*Great hilarity among the* SPECTATORS.]

PRESIDING JUDGE: I shall clear the court.

MIMI [*screams*]: Clear this rubbish. All this rubbish.

[MIMI *exits.*]

PRESIDING JUDGE: Ernestine Puschek is called to the stand.

[ERNESTINE *enters.*]

PRESIDING JUDGE: Your name is Ernestine Puschek.

ERNESTINE: Yes.

PRESIDING JUDGE: A cook by trade. You are aware—

ERNESTINE: Yes.

PRESIDING JUDGE: —of the meaning of an oath.

ERNESTINE: Yes. Yes.

PRESIDING JUDGE: You are testifying to the truth and nothing but the truth.

ERNESTINE: Yes.

PRESIDING JUDGE: Would you like to take the oath with the invocation to God?

ERNESTINE [*very precise*]: Yes, indeed. I swear by Almighty God.

PRESIDING JUDGE: Repeat after me.

[*The oath is administered.*]

PRESIDING JUDGE: You have known the defendant for about ten months.

ERNESTINE: Yes.

PRESIDING JUDGE: When did your relations begin?

ERNESTINE: Yes.

PRESIDING JUDGE: When exactly?

ERNESTINE: It started the very first day.

PRESIDING JUDGE: The defendant seduced you immediately?

ERNESTINE: I fell in love with him immediately.

PRESIDING JUDGE: Had you been with a man before him?

ERNESTINE: No.

PRESIDING JUDGE: Do you have parents? Family?

ERNESTINE: He's the only one.

PRESIDING JUDGE: Then what do you know about the crime?

ERNESTINE: He's the only one I have in the world.

PRESIDING JUDGE: We all understand your pain.

ERNESTINE [*very restrained*]: I would like—

PRESIDING JUDGE: What would you like?

ERNESTINE: I didn't think it would be like this.

PRESIDING JUDGE: What did you think?

ERNESTINE [*tottering*]: I can't.

PRESIDING JUDGE: Do you mean give evidence?

[ERNESTINE *is silent.*]

PRESIDING JUDGE: Unfortunately, the Court has no other means of uncovering the truth.

ERNESTINE: I'd like to go back home.

PRESIDING JUDGE: We cannot dispense with your testimony.

ERNESTINE: I have nothing to say.

PRESIDING JUDGE: We shall try to question you as delicately as we can.

ERNESTINE: God help me.

[ERNESTINE *suddenly sinks down. She is helped up.*]

PRESIDING JUDGE: Get the witness a chair.

PUBLIC PROSECUTOR: The witness's distress will be understandable to any man of feeling.

[ERNESTINE *sits down and stares fixedly at* TUNICHTGUT, *who smiles at her, embarrassed and unsuspecting.*]

PUBLIC PROSECUTOR: She is distinct from that previous witness, a woman who in the most frivolous way mocked all the most sacred institutions of humanity. For she has cause to break down when she sees the man of her choice unmasked as a criminal.

DEFENSE COUNSEL: The public prosecutor is getting ahead of himself. The witness has not said that she takes the defendant to be a criminal.

ERNESTINE [*quietly*]: We are all criminals.

PRESIDING JUDGE: What do you mean by that?

[ERNESTINE *looks at the* PRESIDING JUDGE.]

DEFENSE COUNSEL: Are you referring to the crime of false maternity which you attempted?

PUBLIC PROSECUTOR: That case is still under investigation. I do not presume at this time to admit that your copiously documented great love for the defendant constitutes important extenuating circumstances.

[ERNESTINE *sits motionless.*]

PUBLIC PROSECUTOR: In the meantime, I do not propose to go farther into the question of false maternity until the case against the witness is proven.

DEFENSE COUNSEL: I attribute great importance to that question.

PRESIDING JUDGE: In any event the witness can refuse to answer.

[ERNESTINE *sits motionless.*]

DEFENSE COUNSEL: It has been established that the defendant believed in that child until this very day. The court has noted with disfavor the so-called immoral aspects in the life of the defendant.

[ERNESTINE, *cool and collected, pays close attention.*]

PRESIDING JUDGE: The immorality of a man who thinks it natural to have relations with five women at once is beyond "so-called." That does not prevent us from wondering at the defendant's gullibility.

TUNICHTGUT: You would have been taken in, too, your honor.

PRESIDING JUDGE: We will not let ourselves be taken in here. Bear that in mind.

ERNESTINE [*calmly*]: You can't get taken in.

PRESIDING JUDGE: Do you want to refuse to give evidence in the matter of the attempted false maternity?

ERNESTINE [*rises again, firmly*]: No.

PRESIDING JUDGE: Then explain the motive to us. Did you want the defendant to marry you?

ERNESTINE: No. I didn't care.

PRESIDING JUDGE: Perhaps you don't understand yourself any more.

ERNESTINE: I was never after that. I only wanted him. I can support myself.

PRESIDING JUDGE: What do you mean by that?

ERNESTINE: Nobody has to look after me.

PRESIDING JUDGE: Then why did you forge a doctor's certificate?

ERNESTINE: Because I promised him a baby.

PRESIDING JUDGE: When did you make that promise?

ERNESTINE [*slowly*]: Right at the start.

PRESIDING JUDGE: At the start of your relationship?

ERNESTINE: I didn't want to lie on the first night.

PRESIDING JUDGE: So you promised it to him?

ERNESTINE: I was grateful to God for giving him to me. I was so happy. So I thought, *There's got to be a baby*. Besides, he acted as if he wanted it too. He was already lying to me.

PRESIDING JUDGE: And when no baby came, you considered yourself obligated—

ERNESTINE: I'm not a whore. For me it was everything that we were together. I'm not like all his other women. Why are you looking at me that way?

PRESIDING JUDGE: No one is looking at you.

ERNESTINE: Strip me naked, why don't you?

PRESIDING JUDGE: Who's doing that?

ERNESTINE: I'm ready for anything. Nothing can happen to me.

PRESIDING JUDGE: Would you prefer not to give further testimony on this point.

ERNESTINE Take the chair away.

PRESIDING JUDGE: In what way is the chair suddenly bothering you?

ERNESTINE: I'm not a weakling.

PRESIDING JUDGE: She's feeling faint.

ERNESTINE: It's over. I know what I want.

DEFENSE COUNSEL: Did you know beforehand that you could not have children?

ERNESTINE: I'm not a whore.

PRESIDING JUDGE: You have already answered that to the point.

ERNESTINE: Maybe he's the one that can't have children. He's never had one before.

TUNICHTGUT [*laughs*]: That would have been stupid of me.

ERNESTINE [*calmly*]: But you didn't care if I was the dope?

TUNICHTGUT: Tinchen.

ERNESTINE: I'm not a dope.

PRESIDING JUDGE: Where were you on the day of the crime?

ERNESTINE: That's when I first found out.

PRESIDING JUDGE: What did you find out?

ERNESTINE: That he was cheating on me.

PRESIDING JUDGE: When did you see him?

ERNESTINE: At 7:30.

PRESIDING JUDGE: He came for supper in the kitchen as usual?

ERNESTINE: The mistress knew about it. She wanted to give me money to pay the midwife.

PRESIDING JUDGE: He was arrested in the kitchen. When was the last time you saw him before that?

ERNESTINE: At 6:30.

PRESIDING JUDGE: Where was that?

ERNESTINE: In his room.

PRESIDING JUDGE: Then he left you and didn't say where he was going? Where were you in the meantime?

ERNESTINE: I went shopping. The bills are in the housekeeping book.

PRESIDING JUDGE: Did you run into him on the street?

ERNESTINE: No.

PRESIDING JUDGE: He claims he had gone for a walk. When you returned from shopping, was he already back?

ERNESTINE: He was in the kitchen, flirting with the girl.

PRESIDING JUDGE: What girl?

ERNESTINE: Mimi.

PRESIDING JUDGE: We have made her acquaintance. Did you notice any signs of excitement about him?

ERNESTINE: He was chatting her up hot and heavy. When I left the room, he kissed her.

PRESIDING JUDGE: Didn't something dawn on you then?

ERNESTINE [*quickly*]: I didn't take it seriously.

DEFENSE COUNSEL: So the witness is not normally jealous.

ERNESTINE [*after a pause*]: I wanted to take my revenge later.

PRESIDING JUDGE: You didn't notice any other signs that were out of the ordinary?

ERNESTINE: He didn't have an appetite.

PRESIDING JUDGE: Was he nervous?

ERNESTINE: He had already eaten before, with the Kudelka woman. She'd snatched him away from my cooking too.

DEFENSE COUNSEL: How do you know that?

ERNESTINE [*calmly*]: From the newspapers. Can I go now?

PRESIDING JUDGE: The last time you talked to him, did Kudelka's name come up?

ERNESTINE [*firmly*]: Yes.

PRESIDING JUDGE: Was there talk about her money?

ERNESTINE: Yes.

PRESIDING JUDGE: Did he remark that he wanted to lay hands on her money?

ERNESTINE [*quickly*]: No. He is not a thief.

PRESIDING JUDGE: Because he didn't manage to get hold of all of it.

ERNESTINE: He is not a thief.

PRESIDING JUDGE: They found a hundred marks in his pocket. Did they come from you?

ERNESTINE: No.

PRESIDING JUDGE: Whom did they come from, then?

ERNESTINE: The Kudelka woman.

PRESIDING JUDGE: We found the money drawer open.

ERNESTINE: He is not a thief. He had it off of her. But he's not a thief.

PRESIDING JUDGE: A murderer then?

ERNESTINE [*calmly*]: As God wills.

TUNICHTGUT: Tinchen.

PRESIDING JUDGE: What do you mean by that?

ERNESTINE: God's will be done. I've settled accounts with him.

PRESIDING JUDGE: Settled accounts with whom?

ERNESTINE: And with life.

PRESIDING JUDGE: In what way have you settled accounts with him?

ERNESTINE: I'm done.

PRESIDING JUDGE: You mean to say that you are reconciled to your fate?

ERNESTINE: He's done too. Can I go now?

PRESIDING JUDGE: What do you have to say to the witness's remarks?

TUNICHTGUT [*casually*]: The good Lord is looking out for me.

ERNESTINE [*looks at him, calmly*]: Good-bye.

PRESIDING JUDGE [*to* PUBLIC PROSECUTOR]: Have you any more questions for the witness.

TUNICHTGUT: You don't really believe I murdered her?

PUBLIC PROSECUTOR: No.

TUNICHTGUT: Or do you have an objection to that as well?

PRESIDING JUDGE: Does the defense have another question?

TUNICHTGUT: Why don't you open your mouth?

ERNESTINE [*calmly*]: I will always have you in my thoughts. [*To the* PRESIDING JUDGE.] May I leave?

TUNICHTGUT [*aghast*]: You really believe it?

PRESIDING JUDGE: Answer the defendant's question.

TUNICHTGUT [*recklessly*]: Don't stick your nose into everything.

PRESIDING JUDGE [*jumps up*]: The defendant hasn't the slightest conception of the plight he's in.

TUNICHTGUT [*affectionately*]: Goldilocks, answer me.

[ERNESTINE'*s composure gives out; she sinks back onto the chair.*]

PRESIDING JUDGE: The court will impose an exemplary penalty for the incessant contempt of court.

[*Tumul among the* SPECTATORS.]

TUNICHTGUT: I never would have expected it of you. [*Strokes* ERNESTINE'*s face.*] Let them say what they want.

ERNESTINE: I never would have expected it of you either. Now we can both believe it.

[*The* PRESIDING JUDGE *and the* ADDITIONAL JUDGES *have deliberated briefly.*]

PRESIDING JUDGE: The court has completed its deliberation.

[ERNESTINE *and* TUNICHTGUT *are parted by the* COURT OFFICER, *without their taking any notice of what is going on.*]

DEFENSE COUNSEL: I object to the suspension of the testimony.

TUNICHTGUT: I'm sorry. When all's said and done, I'm a sensation.

ERNESTINE [*nods*]: A sensation, yeah.

PRESIDING JUDGE: The court cannot tolerate this incessant insubordination. The court is perfectly legal.

[*The* PRESIDING JUDGE *and the* ADDITIONAL JUDGES *exit.*]

TUNICHTGUT: Are you still mad at me?

ERNESTINE [*laughs maliciously*]: You old smoothie.

TUNICHTGUT: Yes?

ERNESTINE [*pauses*]: Never mind. Which one was number four?

TUNICHTGUT: Number four?

ERNESTINE: The Kudelka woman, the maid at the hotel, and Frieda from next door I found out about. But the papers say that you had four at the same time.

TUNICHTGUT: The papers always exaggerate.

CLERK OF THE COURT: Please do not converse with the defendant.

ERNESTINE: They said it here too.

TUNICHTGUT: You were my one and only.

ERNESTINE: Now you're fibbing again. I was number five.

CLERK OF THE COURT: I'll have to remove the witness.

TUNICHTGUT [*looks around*]: Is it over? Where did the judges go?

ERNESTINE: So you won't tell me who number four was?

[*The* PRESIDING JUDGE *and the* ADDITIONAL JUDGES *return.*]

PRESIDING JUDGE: The defendant is sentenced to a penalty of ten days' imprisonment for incessant breach of the peace. Does the witness have anything more to say?

ERNESTINE [*very precisely*]: No.

PRESIDING JUDGE: Does the defendant have a question to put to the witness?

TUNICHTGUT: No.

PRESIDING JUDGE: The defense counsel's objection is overruled.

TUNICHTGUT: We had our say already.

ERNESTINE [*calmly*]: Good-bye, Gustav.

PRESIDING JUDGE: I conclude the hearing of witnesses.

TUNICHTGUT: There is no number four. [*Laughs.*]

PRESIDING JUDGE: The public prosecutor has the floor.

[*The large assize courtroom goes dark.*]

[*Courtroom 3 lights up.* OLGA NAGERLE's *case continues.* PRESIDING JUDGE; ADDITIONAL JUDGES; PUBLIC PROSECUTOR.]

PRESIDING JUDGE: The public prosecutor has the floor.

PUBLIC PROSECUTOR [*rises*]: I shall be brief. This trial has shed light on the depravity of that segment of our population which is specially chosen to be our hope for the future. I mean the younger generation. The case of Olga Nagerle is not unique. Abortion and infanticide have become the common recourse of the female portion of all classes of society. The irresponsible propaganda of so-called enlightened circles even advances the work of destruction. Here the harshest punishment would be too mild. What is punishment? Only naïve popular sentiment takes it to be a disguised form of revenge and retaliation. But the State has nothing to avenge, its job is to warn and defend. The concept of the State would lose any meaning—

[*Courtroom 3 goes dark.*]

[*Courtroom 1 lights up.* Proceedings against ALFRED FISCHAU. DEFENSE COUNSEL.]

DEFENSE COUNSEL [*continuing his plea*]: —the concept of the State would lose any meaning if it were destroy the future of such a worthy young man as Alfred Fischau. Popular sentiment— which only an ignorant theoretician could call naïve, but which, in reality, expresses with magnificent intuition the instinctual, elementary will to life—popular sentiment has long ago lost any sense of what punishment means, for its application has congealed into firmly preestablished norms, and there are countless crimes which it actually cannot reach. Here a young man has erred out of passion—but with so honorable, so open a face that whoever calls this young man a criminal may himself be committing a crime. What is a criminal? We cannot answer this question. Only this much is certain—many of those whom the State sends to prison are far from being criminals. This much is certain—many of those whom the State allows to run around freely and honorably are criminals. Where is the connection between a crime and a punishment, if the way the law is interpreted can result in different outcomes? Is there any court in Germany that will pass the same judgment in a criminal case as any other court in Germany? And yet they both speak for justice and law. Here we stand before the eternally closed portal: What is justice if it is not humane? What is the essence of justice—?

[*Courtroom 1 goes dark.*]

[*The judges' reading room lights up.* YOUNGER JUDGE *and* OLDER JUDGE.]

YOUNGER JUDGE: What is the essence of justice?

OLDER JUDGE [*smiles*]: Even if the light coming through the window on this rainy day weren't so dim, I would recognize at once from the question that you are young, colleague. Forget about it. The essence of justice is as undefinable as the essence of life or electricity, if you will. We can know only their application.

YOUNGER JUDGE: Electricity is a force of nature, independent of our will. But justice is a creation of the intellect, a theorem, commonly accepted, subject to our will, our laws, a bit like mathematics.

OLDER JUDGE: And therein lies the curse of its ambiguity. If we take justice to be mathematical, then it will be unsuitable for human life. Then is it a force of nature? Yes. A force of nature, which always blows our intellectual conceptions to kingdom come. We hold on tight to these intellectual conceptions as long as we can. That is our only salvation.

YOUNGER JUDGE: And what if they collapse?

OLDER JUDGE: Then it's sheer anarchy.

YOUNGER JUDGE: The ideal state is still a confederation of millions of people, who at bottom are living next to one another in a state of anarchy. We have carefully cemented it with conventions—but are they anything more than an outer fence made up of formal acts of courtesy, respectability, compulsory morality, and exactly calculated tokens of respect?

OLDER JUDGE: What about the nation?

YOUNGER JUDGE: At given moments we suddenly experience a feeling of solidarity—at moments of great, common danger. You call that a nation? Cows in a pasture have the same feeling of solidarity when there's a thunderstorm.

OLDER JUDGE: The brotherhood of man presupposes the existence of law.

YOUNGER JUDGE: And yet I have observed such a brotherhood firmly established only when this law is broken, when we are talking about criminals. The negative form of life is that of apathetic, egocentric neighbors, the lookers-on, the uncaring. Those are the only real crimes, because they originate in unfeeling hearts, inert minds—in other words, the uttermost denial of the life force and the idea of solidarity. These crimes, however, go unpunished. The other kind of felonious actions are manifestations of the life force, and therefore positive, but in all proven cases are punished as crimes. That's when a human being carves into his own flesh and calls it "Law." That's when the People castrates its own living body and always "in the name of the People."

[*The judges' reading room remains lit.*]

[*Courtroom 3 lights up. Sentencing in the case of* OLGA NAGERLE. PRESIDING JUDGE; ADDITIONAL JUDGES; KUMMERER; OLGA.]

[*Everyone stands.*]

PRESIDING JUDGE [*severely*]: In the name of the People! The defendant Olga Nagerle is convicted of manslaughter and sentenced to eight years and seven months' imprisonment.

KUMMERER: For the love of God.

[KUMMERER *takes* OLGA *in his arms*.]

[*The* PRESIDING JUDGE *and the* ADDITIONAL JUDGES *exit. Courtroom 3 remains lit.*]

[*The judges' reading room.*]

OLDER JUDGE [*has been walking up and down*]: Perhaps [*smiling*] . . . perhaps you are right insofar as it is a mysterious law of nature. We are all subject to the great law of self-destruction.

[*The judges' reading room remains lit.*]

[*Courtroom 2 lights up. Verdict in the* SCHIMMELWEIS *case.* PRESIDING JUDGE; ADDITIONAL JUDGES; DEFENSE COUNSEL; IMMANUEL SCHIMMELWEIS; FRANK; OTTFRIED.]

[*Everyone stands.*]

PRESIDING JUDGE [*severely*]: In the name of the People! The defendant Immanuel Schimmelweis is acquitted of the charge of blackmail, with court costs charged to the State.

DEFENSE COUNSEL: Congratulations, Herr Schimmelweis.

[*The* PRESIDING JUDGE *and the* ADDITIONAL JUDGES *exit.*]

SCHIMMELWEIS: Good afternoon, gentlemen. I'm off.

[SCHIMMELWEIS *exits*.]

FRANK: Ottfried!

[OTTFRIED *sneaks out*.]

[*Courtroom 2 remains lit.*]

[*The judges' reading room.*]

YOUNGER JUDGE: If it is a law of nature for us to commit so-called acts of destruction, why should we punish them as crimes?

[*The judges' reading room remains lit.*]

[*Courtroom 1 lights up.*]

[*Sentencing in the Fischau case.* PRESIDING JUDGE; ADDITIONAL JUDGES; ALFRED FISCHAU; ALFRED FISCHAU'S MOTHER.]

[*Everyone stands.*]

PRESIDING JUDGE [*severely*]: In the name of the People! Allowing for extenuating circumstances, the defendant Alfred Fischau is sentenced for grand larceny to five months' imprisonment. The court has decided to suspend the sentence for a period of probation.

ALFRED: Mother! [*Falls into her arms.*]

[*The* PRESIDING JUDGE *and the* ADDITIONAL JUDGES *exit.*]

[*Courtroom 1 remains lit.*]

[*The judges' reading room.*]

OLDER JUDGE: Your questions have quite intrigued me. I love this sort of conversation before meals. But neither of us can explain anything.

YOUNGER JUDGE: Nevertheless, it's disturbing that in many cases, such as blackmail, revenge, the penal law is used to encourage crime.

OLDER JUDGE: Everything that somehow stirs the mind always conceals a bit of a mystery. Not only is it what created the world, but which dictates the slightest human feelings, hour by hour.

YOUNGER JUDGE: How can you speak of feelings and then pass judgment on them as crimes?

OLDER JUDGE: Forget about it. It's a matter of habit. [*Takes his overcoat and hat.*] After all, what is a crime?

YOUNGER JUDGE: I believe we will never get to the bottom of things until we do away with this term.

OLDER JUDGE: Let's go home. It's late.

[*The judges' reading room remains lit.*]

[*Large assize courtroom lights up. Sentencing in the* TUNICHTGUT *case.* PRESIDING JUDGE; ADDITIONAL JUDGES; TUNICHTGUT; DEFENSE COUNSEL; ERNESTINE.]

PRESIDING JUDGE [*severely*]: In the name of the People! The defendant Gustav Tunichtgut is sentenced to death on the charge of murder, to be preceded by three weeks' imprisonment for inveterate contempt of court.

TUNICHTGUT [*howls*]: Stinking assholes! The lot of you!

[TUNICHTGUT *flings himself at the* PRESIDING JUDGE.]

PRESIDING JUDGE: Remove this man.

[*The* PRESIDING JUDGE *and the* ADDITIONAL JUDGES *exit.*]

DEFENSE COUNSEL [*to* TUNICHTGUT]: Calm down. We'll file an appeal.

[ERNESTINE *has fainted. She is helped up.*]

[*The large assize courtroom remains lit.*]

[*The judges' reading room.*]

YOUNGER JUDGE: If we let ourselves get into the habit of looking on while people are destroyed without doing something about it—what's the use of thinking?

OLDER JUDGE: The quicker you dismiss this question, the happier you'll be in this world.

[*The* YOUNGER JUDGE *takes his overcoat and hat.*]

[*All the areas are lit. The defendants are segregated from the* SPECTATORS. *Life goes on.*]

[*Curtain.*]

ACT III

Apartment house from act I

[*The music of a jazz band playing a Charleston, muted, is audible for a while. Area 5,* FRAU BERLESSEN's *living room, lights up.*]

[JOSEF; OTTFRIED.]

JOSEF: How much do you want for yourself?

OTTFRIED: Ten percent.

JOSEF: That's almost four thousand marks, man!

OTTFRIED: Then forget it.

JOSEF: Now he shows his claws. [*Laughs.*] And I took you for a sensitive dreamer-boy.

OTTFRIED: I was once.

JOSEF: Your pale little face, your slender frame are a dangerous con game.

OTTFRIED [*laughs*]: Don't get too graphic.

JOSEF: I'm learning. There can be angel faces with no scruples.

OTTFRIED: That's what you've got talons for. We complement one another.

JOSEF: Lack of scruples is not learned, it's innate. Even blond curls can cover rotting meat.

OTTFRIED: Your compliments are certainly unique.

JOSEF: Variety is the spice of life. [*Whistles the Charleston with the band.*]

OTTFRIED: The two of us could put the world in our pocket—

JOSEF [*looks at* OTTFRIED]: The two of us?

OTTFRIED: —if we stick together. Above all: Get out of this building. It's compromised.

JOSEF: There are few buildings in this world that aren't. You don't dare look in any window. I'm comfortable here.

OTTFRIED: The proximity of our disreputable families—speaking as a businessman—is bound to blacken our good reputations.

JOSEF [*laughs*]: The gentleman on probation is moving out of his furnished room today, and straight to America.

OTTFRIED: A certain lady is already waiting for him in Hamburg.

JOSEF: And your worthy lady mama is recovering under palm trees on the Riviera. What more do you want? A year from now nobody will be talking about it. The spice of life. [*Calls into the kitchen.*] Ernestine!

[ERNESTINE *enters.*]

JOSEF: The ladies will be here any minute. Carla should set the table.

[ERNESTINE *exits.*]

OTTFRIED: You're expecting company?

JOSEF: Two ladies. You'd like them. Would you care to stay?

OTTFRIED: No, thank you very much. I have an appointment.

JOSEF: I understand. [*Laughs.*] You have exclusive tastes.

OTTFRIED [*annoyed*]: We'll seal the deal tomorrow morning.

JOSEF: You can't wait?

OTTFRIED [*defiantly*]: You think I'm afraid?

JOSEF: Just don't be crude.

OTTFRIED: Do you think I'm afraid?

JOSEF [*crudely*]: What do I care whether you're afraid?

OTTFRIED: If I don't have your signature by 10:00 tomorrow morning, I'll take the deal somewhere else.

JOSEF: Down, boy.

OTTFRIED [*disconcerted*]: What did you say?

JOSEF: So far as I'm concerned, you're wet behind the ears. I make deals like this every day.

OTTFRIED: But you can't make this one without me.

JOSEF: Pull in your claws.

OTTFRIED: And you, your talons. We're better off if we're on good terms.

[CARLA KOCH, *twenty-one years old, enters and sets the table.*]

JOSEF [*to* OTTFRIED]: Do you recognize the silver? Your bosom buddy pawned it.

OTTFRIED [*laughs*]: You mean your brother.

JOSEF: The kid shows decidedly criminal tendencies. [*To* CARLA.] You should put the wineglasses on the right.

OTTFRIED [*suddenly*]: Wasn't that the door?

JOSEF: That'll be Frank.

OTTFRIED [*quickly*]: See you tomorrow.

JOSEF: You're avoiding him?

OTTFRIED: There's no point in seeing him.

[OTTFRIED *Exits.*]

JOSEF: Where were you in service before that you put wineglasses on the left?

[CARLA *is silent.*]

JOSEF: Wineglasses always go on the right.

[CARLA *is silent.*]

JOSEF: Answer me.

CARLA [*subdued*]: The master shouldn't beller at me like that.

JOSEF [*teasing her*]: I shouldn't *what* at you?

CARLA: Please.

JOSEF: And what if I do beller at you? Where does one put the wineglasses?

CARLA [*subjugated*]: On the right.

JOSEF: On the right of what?

CARLA: The master also shouldn't try and break down my door at night.

JOSEF: You're crazy.

CARLA: I don't let just anybody in.

JOSEF: Since when am I just anybody?

CARLA: I only want the master to know that.

JOSEF: That I'm just anybody? I don't know that. Stand still when you're talking to me.

CARLA: I have to set the table.

JOSEF: And what if I don't know that?

CARLA: I'm not a streetwalker.

JOSEF [*embraces* CARLA]: What if I don't know that?

CARLA [*hardly so subdued*]: The master shouldn't grab me.

JOSEF: You're not a streetwalker?

CARLA: The master should let me go.

JOSEF: Here, to stop your mouth. [*Kisses* CARLA.]

[CARLA *slaps* JOSEF'*s face and pulls free.*]

JOSEF [*laughs*]: I like it.

CARLA [*beside herself*]: Is nothing sacred to you?

JOSEF: Absolutely nothing. A kiss here on the cheek, you devil. It's burning there.

CARLA: To have to work for someone like you.

JOSEF: Why did nature make you so pretty?

CARLA: That's no reason I should give myself to you right away.

JOSEF: Everything gives itself to me that comes my way. Why did nature make you so pretty? I'll knock on your door tomorrow too.

CARLA: I'll scratch your eyes out.

JOSEF: You can try it out on me in your quiet little bedroom.

CARLA [*desperately*]: I'm not free.

JOSEF: What pretty girl is free?

CARLA: You must count on that.

JOSEF: You've got funny ideas. Your predecessor was cleverer than that. She has her own apartment, three friends and someone to teach her manners.

CARLA: I don't want three friends, I only want one.

JOSEF: Who's a poor sucker?

[CARLA *is silent.*]

JOSEF: Then what is he?

[CARLA *is silent.*]

JOSEF: A poor sucker then.

CARLA: With money, your kind can buy everything.

JOSEF [*laughs*]: Even you.

CARLA [*explodes*]: Stop picking on me.

JOSEF [*laughs*]: I wasn't picking on you.

CARLA: He's a boxer.

JOSEF [*uncertain*]: A boxer?

CARLA: If he finds out about this, he'll break you in half.

JOSEF [*cautiously*]: First someone has to tell him.

CARLA: So you watch your step.

JOSEF [*provoking*]: What are you going to tell him? Prove it first. I still need a parlor maid.

[JOSEF *is about to go.*]

CARLA [*very hesitant*]: That's not what I meant.

JOSEF [*listens*]: Go back to the kitchen.

CARLA: All right. [*Awkwardly.*] Naturally, I won't tell him.

JOSEF [*sharply*]: Why aren't you going to the kitchen?

CARLA [*not moving*]: I am going.

JOSEF: Am I supposed to put my hand in my pocket? No blackmail—
I'm proof against that.

CARLA [*quietly*]: I can't figure out what to do.

JOSEF [*closer*]: Say what?

CARLA [*drained*]: I can't go on living.

JOSEF: Everyone has the opportunity to rise in the world. You're
letting yours slip away. Too bad.

CARLA [*explodes*]: I need money, lots of money.

JOSEF: That's obvious. Go to him.

CARLA: He doesn't have any.

JOSEF: A poor sucker?

CARLA: He was disqualified.

JOSEF: A poor boxer. Then why did you make this scene? You can
always go begging.

CARLA [*indignant*]: I will not beg.

JOSEF: It's bound to happen.

CARLA: I'd rather drown myself.

JOSEF: That's bound to happen too. How much do you need?

CARLA: Give me the money, I'll work two months without pay.

JOSEF: So how much do you need?

CARLA: At least fifty marks.

JOSEF [*laughs*]: You're coming on strong!

CARLA: Help me.

JOSEF: Such an innocent slut.

CARLA: I'll work two months without pay.

JOSEF: In two months you will have earned it anyway.

CARLA: But I need it right now.

JOSEF: Obviously.

CARLA: I want to go on being a respectable girl. Help me!

[CARLA *goes on her knees*.]

JOSEF: Nobody's preventing you.

CARLA: Help me, for heaven's sake.

JOSEF: If it wasn't for your scenes, I could have saved the cost of two ladies today.

CARLA: I can't go on living.

JOSEF: Tomorrow night we'll see if you can.

CARLA: You're treating me abominably.

JOSEF: Call it what you like.

CARLA [*dully*]: I'd like to murder you.

JOSEF [*laughs*]: Try it tomorrow.

CARLA [*on her feet*]: If he learns about it, I'll kill myself.

JOSEF: That boxer better not cross my path.

CARLA: Not that you'd know.

JOSEF: Get back in the kitchen.

[JOSEF *exits*.]

CARLA: He's the only one I love.

[CARLA *stares after* JOSEF *without moving*.]
[*The scene goes dark*.]
[*Jazz band, muted*.]

[*Area 1,* FRAU VON WIEG*'s room, beautified, lights up.*]

[OTTFRIED.]

[FRANK *enters.*]

OTTFRIED: My, you startled me.

FRANK: Why have you been avoiding me?

OTTFRIED: Who's avoiding you?

FRANK: You think I don't see you?

OTTFRIED: I have plenty of other things to do.

FRANK: Just now you were at our place.

OTTFRIED: Incidentally, Liselotte sends you her love.

FRANK: Thanks.

OTTFRIED: She's having a wonderful time. South America is the land of the future, she writes.

FRANK: Have you heard anything?

OTTFRIED: I'm not concerned with those things.

FRANK: Have you seen Schimmelweis again?

OTTFRIED: Barely. It may very well be that South America is the land of the future. Think of the vast prairies, still waiting for human beings. She writes that her husband has a gigantic ranch—

FRANK: In the meantime, have you seen him?

OTTFRIED: Dietrich?

FRANK: Schimmelweis.

OTTFRIED: Will you leave me in peace with your Schimmelweis.

FRANK: So you don't know anything?

OTTFRIED: What am I supposed to know?

FRANK: You know perfectly well what you're supposed to know.

OTTFRIED: Is that why you dropped by?

FRANK: Certainly not to hear that South America is the land of the future.

OTTFRIED: Then I have to tell you that I find South America much more interesting. I am now about to transact a big deal between your brother and my uncle—I mean my brother-in-law. [*Laughs.*] It amounts to the same thing.

FRANK: What amounts to the same thing?

OTTFRIED: My uncle is my brother-in-law.

FRANK: What's my connection with your uncle?

OTTFRIED: Nobody said there is one.

FRANK: Do you mean to say that I should go to your uncle?

OTTFRIED: I've never dreamed of such a thing.

FRANK: Anyhow, I should get away from here.

OTTFRIED: I can write to him.

FRANK: How long will it take?

OTTFRIED: A fortnight.

FRANK: Do you think I really still have a fortnight?

OTTFRIED: Why shouldn't you have a fortnight?

FRANK [*explodes*]: What fantasies are you concocting?

OTTFRIED [*coldly*]: You're going too far for me.

FRANK: You know very well that I can be arrested at any moment.

OTTFRIED: I explained to you before the trial that I don't get involved in such things.

FRANK: You advised me in everything. Ottfried, you didn't stir from my side.

OTTFRIED: Because I was afraid you would do something stupid.

FRANK: I did do something stupid.

OTTFRIED: I was afraid you would take your life.

FRANK: You were afraid that I would give evidence against Schimmelweis.

OTTFRIED [*brutally*]: Now I'm going to throw you out. Advice? We tossed for it because I couldn't put up with your nerves any more.

FRANK: When did we toss for it?

OTTFRIED: We wagered heads or tails, just before you went into court. With a two-mark coin. Do you deny that too?

FRANK: I don't deny it.

OTTFRIED: You call that giving advice? You surprise me.

FRANK: We bet heads or tails as a last resort. Because I continued to distrust your advice.

OTTFRIED [*laughs*]: No one will believe that.

FRANK: But you know it well enough.

OTTFRIED: If a person commits perjury on a coin toss, then whatever the circumstances, he deserves to go to prison.

[FRANK *throws himself at* OTTFRIED.]

OTTFRIED [*holding* FRANK *tight*]: Shall I have you arrested on the spot?

FRANK: That might be the best thing.

OTTFRIED: Sit down and come to your senses.

FRANK: So we played heads or tails for fun.

OTTFRIED: To keep your mind off things.

FRANK: And you quoted the law to me for fun too.

OTTFRIED: So you'd be informed. Do people quote the penal code if they want to play heads or tails? You're incredible.

FRANK: I'm no match for you.

OTTFRIED: I've proved my friendship well enough. Better than some.

FRANK: Whom do you mean?

OTTFRIED: I won't name names.

FRANK: I dare you.

OTTFRIED: I mean the one who turned his pretty backside on you as soon as things smelled fishy.

FRANK: Leave Oskar out of it. What do you know about Oskar?

OTTFRIED: That he's hanging out now with a little Englishman.

FRANK [*beside himself*]: I didn't ask you for tittle-tattle.

OTTFRIED: You asked me what I know about Oskar.

FRANK: I won't let you sully his name.

OTTFRIED: Don't get excited.

FRANK: I simply expressed my disdain because you haven't a clue what love means.

OTTFRIED: Then that's all right.

FRANK: I didn't ask you what Oskar is doing now, but I said, "What do *you* know about Oskar?" Which means I was putting you in your place.

OTTFRIED: I get you.

FRANK: I want you to take it back. If I want to know something about Oskar, you're the last person I'd ask.

OTTFRIED: You can naturally ask him.

FRANK [*explodes*]: Naturally I will ask him. But I don't want to know.

OTTFRIED: Then naturally you won't ask him.

FRANK: Anyway, Oskar is definitely not hanging out with some little Englishman. It's more likely that the little Englishman isn't giving Oskar a moment's peace. And if I wanted to see Oskar, I only have to say so. He'd drop everything for me. Why have you suddenly gone so quiet?

OTTFRIED: I have noticed that things go more smoothly when I let you talk and act as if I'm listening.

FRANK [*jumps up*]: At any rate, I've said what I have to say to you.

OTTFRIED [*uneasy*]: If I can help in any way—

FRANK: No, thanks.

OTTFRIED: You know my situation. Mama's difficulties—

FRANK: And yet you earn a lot of money?

OTTFRIED: A man has to live on something.

FRANK: You've furnished the place very prettily.

OTTFRIED: Temporarily. After Mama returns, I shall rent my own apartment.

FRANK: Congratulations.

OTTFRIED: To the detriment of my art historical studies, which I shall have to give up.

FRANK: You can't have everything.

OTTFRIED: Of course it comes down to fundamentals.

FRANK: To what?

OTTFRIED: To fundamentals. Why are you looking at me like that? Today I'll write to Uncle Dietrich.

FRANK: I'll put an end to this, one way or another.

OTTFRIED [*elusively*]: And you would like to go to South America...?

FRANK: You do say that it's the land of the future. [*Suddenly.*] How much does the voyage cost?

OTTFRIED: I'll have to inquire.

FRANK: The fact is, I have made over two-thirds of what I own to Josef.

OTTFRIED [*laughs*]: Josef really needs your money.

FRANK: He has redeemed the silver. You knew that. Ah, then you didn't know?

OTTFRIED: Your brother reveals only a minuscule sense of family.

FRANK [*sees two teacups on the table*]: Are you expecting someone for tea?

OTTFRIED: A business acquaintance.

FRANK [*after a pause*]: Perhaps I don't actually need to go away?

OTTFRIED: It is quite possible that your fears are exaggerated.

FRANK: Perhaps my testimony won't be investigated any further. Suppose they don't suspect anything?

OTTFRIED: Could be.

FRANK: What could be?

OTTFRIED [*curtly*]: You're right.

FRANK [*pause*]: Good-bye.

OTTFRIED [*brightly*]: See you soon.

FRANK [*pause*]: Will you give me your hand?

OTTFRIED: How can you ask?

[OTTFRIED *and* FRANK *clasp hands.*]

[FRANK *exits.*]

[*Area 1 goes dark.*]

[*Jazz band, muted.*]

[*Area 4,* ALFRED's *room, lights up.* ALFRED *is closing packed suitcases.*]

[FRANK *enters.*]

FRANK: Sorry.

ALFRED [*quietly*]: Frank.

FRANK: I didn't know you were here.

[FRANK *is about to leave again.*]

ALFRED: Do come in.

FRANK: Josef is getting ready for his orgy in the living room.

ALFRED: Close the door behind you. My train is leaving in half an hour.

FRANK [*pauses*]: Good luck to you, Alfred.

ALFRED: I wish you were as happy as I am. The verdict saved my life.

FRANK: Congratulations.

ALFRED: You were on trial too?

FRANK: Only as a witness, not worth mentioning.

ALFRED: I was so taken up with my own concerns. [*Quietly.*] Are you mad at me?

[FRANK *comes closer to* ALFRED.]

ALFRED: Frank!

[ALFRED *and* FRANK *spontaneously embrace.*]

ALFRED: You're trembling.

FRANK: Don't say a word. I have done you a great injustice. In your arms I feel back in our carefree, absurdly carefree childhood.

ALFRED: Why have we made things so hard for ourselves?

FRANK: Oh, life. How old we've grown.

[FRANK *and* ALFRED *break apart.*]

ALFRED: I thought a lot about it during the interrogation.

FRANK [*in full control*]: Tell me.

ALFRED: I love you, Frank.

FRANK: About the interrogation.

ALFRED [*quickly*]: I can't talk about it.

FRANK: Was it awful?

ALFRED: Why are you so interested?

FRANK: Maybe I'll have to go through it myself.

ALFRED: Frank. Who knows when we'll meet again.

FRANK: No one.

ALFRED: Don't you trust me?

FRANK [*calmly*]: My feelings are different from yours and other men. I feel nothing for women. It's against the law. I've broken this law—should I go on? I've fallen into the hands of a blackmailer, who knows everything and forced me to swear that he is not a blackmailer. I also had to swear that I am not a homo.

ALFRED: You could have refused to testify.

FRANK: I wouldn't have survived the shame.

ALFRED: There's no shame in that.

FRANK: When these men start asking questions, want explanations for everything and send you to the police physician to have your body examined, when they hound you until you're a goner, all that's left is shame.

ALFRED: There really is no shame in it.

FRANK: For you and me, because we've been through it.

ALFRED: I also bear the shame of having been convicted. But I don't feel ashamed. We have to fight against these concepts of honor. [*Suddenly.*] You should come with me today.

FRANK [*jumping up*]: What are you saying?

ALFRED: Just pack the bare necessities.

FRANK: Right now?

ALFRED: Leave it all behind.

FRANK: I can't.

ALFRED: Drop this self-persecution. It'll end up destroying you.

FRANK: I have an appointment.

ALFRED: With whom? With your friend?

[FRANK *nods.*]

ALFRED: Then we'll drop in on him together.

FRANK: He's at the Café Atlantic every day at 9:30.

ALFRED: That's too late. If you still want to see him—

FRANK: I absolutely have to see him.

ALFRED: Then we'll drive to his place and you can say a quick good-bye. Where does he live?

[FRANK *cannot speak.*]

FRANK: I can only see him at the Café Atlantic at 9:30. He's there every night, with a little Englishman.

ALFRED [*cautiously*]: Have you broken up?

[FRANK *nods*.]

ALFRED: Then what's keeping you here?

FRANK: I have to see him. I sit a few tables away. We haven't actually broken up. I only keep my distance from him. Intimacy with me might make things awkward for him, you understand.

ALFRED: Why do you humiliate yourself this way?

FRANK: I'm an outcast.

ALFRED: That's ridiculous.

FRANK: Today I'm the only one who knows it.

ALFRED: What are you talking about?

FRANK: Soon everyone will know it. You should have seen, for example, how Ottfried behaves to me now.

ALFRED: I've never liked Ottfried. I consider him a criminal.

FRANK [*laughs*]: We're criminals, all right. You already have it in writing. That's what lies in store for me.

ALFRED: I wouldn't let it get the better of me for all that.

FRANK: Like hogs in a slaughterhouse. First a brand on the behind.

ALFRED: Then you should do all you can to keep out of the slaughterhouse.

FRANK: Maybe I'll disappear tomorrow morning.

ALFRED: What are you doing to do before tomorrow morning?

FRANK: 9:30. You know.

ALFRED: I'm worried about you.

FRANK: Of course it might all be my imagination.

ALFRED: Let me paint for you the horrors of an interrogation.

FRANK: You don't have to scare me. I'm scared enough. But now my heart is a thousand times lighter. When you're gone, I'll still be sitting here, dreaming of you.

ALFRED: Come with me, Frank.

FRANK: I shall stay here as long as possible in your atmosphere.

ALFRED: I could postpone my trip till tomorrow morning. You promise you'll come with me tomorrow morning?

FRANK: Don't start that again.

ALFRED: It's clear that you won't be coming with me tomorrow morning.

FRANK: Drop it, will you.

ALFRED: Somehow you want to let it happen. He's not the only thing keeping you here.

FRANK [*goes to sofa*]: Now you're making things up.

ALFRED: The horrors you're afraid of, somehow you're anticipating them. That is the power of so-called atonement that blinds us and paralyzes us. It's in the blood.

FRANK [*smiles*]: Go on talking. I'm stretched out here because it's been a long time since I've felt so comfortable.

ALFRED: Frank?

FRANK: Am I disturbing you?

ALFRED: You're tired.

FRANK: I feel so good. Last month's persecution is finally over. Where was I, for goodness sake?

[ALFRED *sits beside him.*]

FRANK: Don't you have to pack?

ALFRED: I'm ready.

FRANK: And the books?

ALFRED: I wanted you to put them in the briefcase. But I'll leave them to you.

FRANK: Thanks. I've sold all my own books long ago. [*Exhaling.*] Now at last I can read again.

ALFRED: Frank.

FRANK: Tell me stories about our childhood. How can they claim that life begins the day after graduation? The day after graduation is when it stops.

ALFRED [*slight outburst*]: I suspect that we shall never see one another again.

[*The area goes dark.*]

[*Jazz band, muted.*]

[*Area 3,* TUNICHTGUT's *room, lights up.*]

[*Evening twilight. The furniture in the space is hard to see. The room is empty.*]

[*Area 3 goes dark again.*]

[*Music of the jazz band again.*]

[*Area 6, the kitchen, lights up.*]

[ERNESTINE; TUNICHTGUT's DEFENSE COUNSEL.]

DEFENSE COUNSEL: In any event, I expect something to come of it.

ERNESTINE [*very busy*]: You lawyers are always expecting.

DEFENSE COUNSEL: Trust my experience. But you have to help me.

ERNESTINE: In ten minutes I have to put the mayonnaise on the table.

DEFENSE COUNSEL: Let me remind you that the public prosecutor's completely twisted your testimony. And that it's largely based on circumstantial evidence. Furthermore, it is the same public prosecutor who will appear against you for falsification of maternity.

ERNESTINE: Are you angling to be my defense attorney? I don't scare easy.

DEFENSE COUNSEL: You are possessed.

ERNESTINE: Is that a compliment?

DEFENSE COUNSEL: It's impossible to talk to you.

ERNESTINE: Tunichtgut was a different kind of gentleman.

DEFENSE COUNSEL: The same passion you had in procuring him a child is now pushing you to send him to his death.

ERNESTINE [*calmly*]: Me?

DEFENSE COUNSEL: In any event, you do nothing to prevent the execution.

ERNESTINE: It's much better than if I'd shot him on the spot. It's all he deserves.

DEFENSE COUNSEL: What is much better?

ERNESTINE: That you do it, the Court, in the name of the People.

DEFENSE COUNSEL: Even if he had committed the murder, you should bend every effort to win him a pardon.

ERNESTINE: That's what you think. It's got nothing to do with the murder.

DEFENSE COUNSEL: What he's suffered should be enough to satisfy your need for revenge.

ERNESTINE: And I've suffered nothing.

DEFENSE COUNSEL: Nevertheless, his life is in ruins.

ERNESTINE: And mine isn't. I'll always be one step ahead of him. Only I have to know that he's really behind me.

DEFENSE COUNSEL: See reason and read the petition for pardon that I've drawn up for you. Since the Court threw out the appeal today, it's all that's left.

ERNESTINE: First I have to wipe my hands. [*Takes the paper, reads.*] Petition for pardon.

DEFENSE COUNSEL: Put your signature there.

ERNESTINE: But if he wasn't the murderer, why does he need a petition for pardon? [*Puts the paper aside, beats salad cream.*]

DEFENSE COUNSEL: The court is convinced that he's the murderer.

ERNESTINE: What about you?

DEFENSE COUNSEL: The chain of circumstantial evidence was unbroken. But my human feelings lead me to say he's not.

ERNESTINE: Who did it, then?

DEFENSE COUNSEL: Probably one of Kudelka's regular customers, who knew his way around.

ERNESTINE: He was definitely a regular customer of Kudelka.

DEFENSE COUNSEL: She had plenty.

ERNESTINE: He knew his way around, you can be sure of that. [*Tastes contents of bowl.*] You've never had a mayonnaise as good as this. Want a taste?

DEFENSE COUNSEL: No, thanks.

ERNESTINE: Anything else?

DEFENSE COUNSEL: Frau Puschek, I would put my hand in the fire—

ERNESTINE [*opens the oven door*]: Put it in here.

DEFENSE COUNSEL: It's impossible to talk to you.

ERNESTINE: You wanted to put your hand in the fire.

DEFENSE COUNSEL: Will you sign the petition or not?

ERNESTINE: So the hand in the fire was only lawyer's blather. The court proved he did it, clear as day.

DEFENSE COUNSEL: That means nothing.

ERNESTINE: So if even the Court proves things that aren't true, what do you want from me?

DEFENSE COUNSEL: The court is still a very imperfect institution.

ERNESTINE: Then it should keep its trap shut. And not meddle in our affairs. We could have settled things all by ourselves. But if it sticks its nose into everything, let it sort things out on its own.

DEFENSE COUNSEL: Would you like to punish the Court? Or deal with it so that Tunichtgut's life is saved?

ERNESTINE [*maliciously*]: If things reach the point that a person can be innocent and still get it in the neck, why do you put so much stock in life? I'd rather throttle myself by myself. If he's been proven to be the murderer, even when it isn't likely he's the murderer—

DEFENSE COUNSEL: Of course it isn't impossible. It is even probable.

ERNESTINE: Then you're a son of a bitch, too, his own defense lawyer.

DEFENSE COUNSEL: I don't understand.

ERNESTINE: What do you know whether he is or he isn't. Don't bug your eyes at me like that.

DEFENSE COUNSEL: Do you have any suspicions?

ERNESTINE: I would like to talk to a lawyer.

DEFENSE COUNSEL: Speak, for Christ's sake.

ERNESTINE [*angrily*]: Leave our Lord Jesus out of it.

DEFENSE COUNSEL: Ernestine Puschek, do you know anything about the murder of the Kudelka woman?

ERNESTINE: What do you know about our Lord Jesus?

DEFENSE COUNSEL: Don't change the subject.

ERNESTINE: It's His will that things stay this way.

DEFENSE COUNSEL: You've given yourself away.

ERNESTINE: I've given myself away?

DEFENSE COUNSEL: For if there were only the shadow of a doubt—

ERNESTINE: When did I give myself away?

DEFENSE COUNSEL: —say so. You won't have the slightest trouble on its account. I'll bring it up, without mentioning your name.

ERNESTINE: I guess you'd like to mention your name again? Haven't you had enough?

DEFENSE COUNSEL: I will leave no stone unturned.

ERNESTINE: You'd like to be in the papers again.

DEFENSE COUNSEL: Tell what you know, for Christ's sake.

ERNESTINE [*more casually*]: Are you starting again? You must be a Jew.

DEFENSE COUNSEL: What's that got to do with it?

ERNESTINE: I won't tell anything to a Jew.

DEFENSE COUNSEL: I'm not a Jew.

ERNESTINE: All lawyers are Jews. Everybody knows that.

DEFENSE COUNSEL: I'm not a Jew. But if anybody can help your ex-fiancé, it's me.

ERNESTINE: He was never my fiancé.

DEFENSE COUNSEL: Will you leave that dead and buried?

ERNESTINE: I was never his fiancée. Or can a man have five fiancées?

DEFENSE COUNSEL: Look me in the eye.

ERNESTINE [*smiles uncertainly*]: Yes?

DEFENSE COUNSEL: Talk to me as you look me in the eye.

ERNESTINE: Guess.

DEFENSE COUNSEL: The moment is too important.

ERNESTINE [*wavering*]: Is that so? Then you tell the truth. Just get out, so this will be over at last. [*Pauses.*] Or does he want to leave things as they are.

DEFENSE COUNSEL: Who wants to leave things as they are?

ERNESTINE: Lord Jesus, who you were calling on. So I alone will be done with it. And Tunichtgut gets his just deserts. Why are you staring at me like that?

DEFENSE COUNSEL: Will you finally say clearly if you know something or not?

ERNESTINE: Let it stay that way.

DEFENSE COUNSEL: Stay what way?

[ERNESTINE *looks the* DEFENSE COUNSEL *in the eye and suddenly makes a face.*]

DEFENSE COUNSEL: Be reasonable for once. Stay what way?

ERNESTINE [*at length composed again*]: That you're a Jew.

DEFENSE COUNSEL: This is ridiculous.

ERNESTINE If I were you, I wouldn't look in people's eyes.

DEFENSE COUNSEL: This is absurd.

ERNESTINE: That way, something else might come to light.

DEFENSE COUNSEL: What would come to light?

ERNESTINE [*still calm*]: The Jew stuff.

DEFENSE COUNSEL: I'm not a Jew, damn it. How dare you treat me this way?

ERNESTINE: I didn't send for you.

DEFENSE COUNSEL [*takes his hat*]: I leave it to a cleverer man than I am to figure you out.

ERNESTINE: You think he did it too. Or don't you?

DEFENSE COUNSEL: That's not the point.

ERNESTINE: I think anybody could have done it. What do you know, what can you do?

DEFENSE COUNSEL: It is clear to me that I—

ERNESTINE: You don't know anything. Just who are you?

[DEFENSE COUNSEL *tries to leave.*]

ERNESTINE [*excited*]: You're just the same as the rest of us. What Tunichtgut did you could do too.

DEFENSE COUNSEL: I could certainly be propelled into the next world as innocently as Tunichtgut.

ERNESTINE: We shall all meet there.

DEFENSE COUNSEL: Will you sign or not?

ERNESTINE: Don't expect anything from me. [*Tears up the paper.*] Let 'em send him to the next world.

DEFENSE COUNSEL [*beside himself*]: I'll have you locked up.

ERNESTINE [*explodes*]: You think that I'm a pastry board you can waltz all over?

DEFENSE COUNSEL: Who is waltzing all over you?

ERNESTINE: You and him—I've had enough. Down with the Jews.

DEFENSE COUNSEL: This is unheard of.

ERNESTINE: What does a Jew know about the next world?

DEFENSE COUNSEL [*almost shouting*]: How often do I have to tell you I'm not a Jew.

ERNESTINE: That's why you're still a Jew.

DEFENSE COUNSEL: You belong in prison.

ERNESTINE: If it was up to you. That way you'd get back in the papers. But it won't be up to you. It'll be up to Lord Jesus, and he wants things to stay as they are.

DEFENSE COUNSEL: Your behavior is highly suspicious.

ERNESTINE: When you're done I'll wind up the murderer.

DEFENSE COUNSEL: I believe you're capable of it.

ERNESTINE: Should I throw this hot soup in your face?

DEFENSE COUNSEL: Go to hell.

[*The* DEFENSE COUNSEL *exits.*]

ERNESTINE: See you in the next world, counselor.

[*The tension is released, and* ERNESTINE *sinks onto a chair.*]

[CARLA *enters.*]

CARLA: I have to run an errand. Did you hear a whistle?

ERNESTINE [*dully*]: No.

CARLA: What's with you?

ERNESTINE: It's all over.

CARLA: What's all over?

ERNESTINE: Their looking for somebody else. They'll stick to the one they've got.

CARLA: Stop thinking about it all the time.

ERNESTINE: I've been waiting for it. Now I know. I can be sure now.

[CARLA *takes* ERNESTINE *in her arms.*]

CARLA: Frau Ernestine.

ERNESTINE: Let this be a lesson to you. Don't let anybody twist you round his finger.

[CARLA *remains leaning on* ERNESTINE.]

ERNESTINE: Or are you that far gone already?

CARLA [*quietly*]: I'll tell you about it now.

ERNESTINE: Quick, then. I have no time.

CARLA: I'm not going to stay here.

ERNESTINE [*dully, calmly*]: Has he started pestering you?

CARLA: What am I supposed to do? I need money. Didn't you hear a whistle?

ERNESTINE: No.

CARLA: My fellow let me down.

ERNESTINE: They're all swine. It goes on and on. It's your turn now.

[*A whistle.*]

CARLA: Thank God.

[CARLA *hurries out.*]

ERNESTINE: It's your turn now.

[ERNESTINE *picks up the torn pieces of the petition, spreads them out on the table, and reads them calmly.*]

[*Area 6 goes dark.*]

[*Jazz band, very loud.*]

[*Area 7, the backroom of* KUDELKA's *bar, lights up. The new landlord has enlarged and modernized the bar to incorporate the backroom.*]

[*Jazz band; couples dancing.* BEN SIM, *a boxer, at a table.*]

[CARLA *hurries in.*]

CARLA: I can't stay long. We have guests.

BEN SIM: For all I care, you can go now.

CARLA: Don't be rude. Where is the lady?

BEN SIM: She'll be here soon. What's new?

CARLA: Nothing.

BEN SIM: Then it's settled. I've been telling you for a month.

CARLA: You don't have to go through it.

BEN SIM: Just start whining again.

CARLA: It's an operation.

BEN SIM [*laughs*]: It's a procedure, not an operation.

CARLA: And a crime. [*Timidly.*] Don't you want to keep it?

BEN SIM: You're crazy.

CARLA: I'd like to keep it.

BEN SIM: A millstone that's going to hang around your neck forever.

CARLA: I'd go on working.

BEN SIM: No marrying.

CARLA: If you only loved me.

BEN SIM: Crazy. I'm not going to go out with someone who's got an illegitimate kid.

CARLA: But it's yours.

BEN SIM: It's still a disgrace.

CARLA: Better a disgrace than a crime.

BEN SIM: What do you mean by that? There's no crime so long as nobody knows. But a disgrace sticks with you.

CARLA: And if anyone finds out?

BEN SIM: You're in stir a couple weeks, and it's like nothing happened. Just the opposite.

CARLA: The opposite?

BEN SIM: Nowadays it's downright classy.

CARLA: Oh God in heaven.

BEN SIM: What did you order?

CARLA: Nothing.

BEN SIM: Waiter, a slivovitz.

CARLA: And what about money?

BEN SIM: Don't talk so stupid.

CARLA: I gave you all my savings.

BEN SIM: Not much to it. There's all that silver lying around upstairs.

CARLA: Ben.

BEN SIM: Need must feed.

CARLA: First I've got to get rid of the baby—next I'm supposed to steal? What more do you want of me?

[*A* WAITER *brings the slivovitz.*]

BEN SIM: First of all, I don't want anything more of you, and second of all, a lot I care how you get rid of it. You pleaded with me to get a discreet woman, I looked for one, I found one, I sent for one. Am I supposed to do everything? You want her to cut it out of my belly for you?

CARLA [*fearful*]: Do you want me to walk the streets?

BEN SIM: This women stuff makes me puke. [*Drinks.*] Bottoms up!

[*The stage goes dark.*]

[*Jazz band, muted.*]

[*Area 2,* OLGA NAGERLE'*s room, lights up.* KUMMERER *alone, writing.*]

[ERNESTINE *enters.*]

KUMMERER: You remind me of my high school years, my golden age. I was cramming nonstop, and my mother would bring me my meals in my room, as you do every day.

ERNESTINE: What are you writing night and day? You look green.

KUMMERER [*smiles*]: One day it will be a book titled *There Are No Criminals*.

ERNESTINE: Forget about all that crap.

KUMMERER: Anyone who suffered as Olga has is no criminal.

ERNESTINE: If only I hadn't promised to take the kid. It's my fault. Let me have another sleeping powder.

KUMMERER: Didn't I buy you a whole tube of Veronal yesterday?

ERNESTINE [*nods*]: I lost it.

KUMMERER: Here—one tablet.

[ERNESTINE *snatches away the whole bottle of Veronal.*]

KUMMERER: All you need is one tablet.

ERNESTINE: I need a lot more.

KUMMERER: You'd better watch out, it's a 30 milligram dose.

ERNESTINE: And what if I took all of them?

KUMMERER [*laughs*]: Then you'd be dead.

ERNESTINE [*laughs*]: Then I'd be dead?

KUMMERER [*laughs*]: On the spot.

ERNESTINE [*laughs*]: Taste the mayonnaise.

KUMMERER: I know what a good cook you are.

ERNESTINE: I've got one thousand, four hundred sixty marks in the savings bank. Here's the book.

KUMMERER: What am I supposed to do with it?

ERNESTINE [*laughs*]: How long do I have to bottle-feed you? Try to figure things out for yourself.

KUMMERER: I don't understand.

ERNESTINE [*laughs*]: You are, after all, the father of my child. Take the bankbook. [*Stares at* KUMMERER *a long time.*] Good-bye.

[ERNESTINE *suddenly exits.*]

KUMMERER: Frau Puschek, your bankbook.

ERNESTINE [*offstage*]: Don't you dare come downstairs and look for me.

[KUMMERER *goes on writing.*]

[*The stage goes dark.*]

[*Jazz band, very muted.*]

[*Area 3,* TUNICHTGUT'*s room, lights up.*]

[DEFENSE COUNSEL; FISTELKREUZ, *the building custodian.*]

DEFENSE COUNSEL [*sits, taking notes*]: The bed.

FISTELKREUZ: Eiderdown it ain't.

DEFENSE COUNSEL: What would it go for?

FISTELKREUZ: Sprucewood, sir.

DEFENSE COUNSEL: I'll put down thirty marks.

FISTELKREUZ: You can live in hope.

DEFENSE COUNSEL: I've had over eight hundred marks in heavy costs.

FISTELKREUZ: That kind of trial is expensive.

DEFENSE COUNSEL: The court costs alone. I'm not even talking about my fee.

FISTELKREUZ: It made you famous, sir.

DEFENSE COUNSEL: This rubbish won't bring a hundred marks.

FISTELKREUZ: Hardly. It's a pity about the man. Just thinking about it.

DEFENSE COUNSEL: We bang our heads against the wall over the future of mankind. In the end, not thinking is the only salvation.

FISTELKREUZ: When I put out the light at night, I'm scared of my shadow. Is it a comfort that it was his first murder?

DEFENSE COUNSEL: Put your trust in human law.

FISTELKREUZ: Otherwise you'd have to throw yourself off the roof.

DEFENSE COUNSEL: That's why it was created. As a comfort for those who don't run afoul of it.

FISTELKREUZ: Even so I feel a noose around my neck.

DEFENSE COUNSEL: But reason tells you you have nothing to fear.

FISTELKREUZ: I still can't sleep at night.

DEFENSE COUNSEL: My good sir, there you touch on the deepest question of our existence. What would come of authority if our reason were able to govern our feelings? However much reason tells you that nothing can happen to you, it was him, not you, who committed a murder. You feel his noose around your neck.

FISTELKREUZ: Don't you?

DEFENSE COUNSEL: I do. The more a man has learned to think, the stronger the feeling. This contradiction is what protects us against the world. It's the grain of salt of life. If we could in fact live according to reason, we would all be dead long ago. Murder and crime are the indispensable manure from which we spring.

FISTELKREUZ: A man could lose his mind.

DEFENSE COUNSEL: The thoughts you are having, Herr Fistelkreuz, result from the imminent execution. The poor devil has made everyone around him think, merely on the grounds of emotion. That is the consequence of any catastrophe.

FISTELKREUZ: Are you saying we shouldn't think?

DEFENSE COUNSEL: We have to think so that we realize we are not leading an animal existence. But thinking, and thinking to the end, are two essentially different matters. To think is to live. To think to the end means death. In a week you'll be able to sleep again. If someone wanted to think to the end, he could never sleep again.

FISTELKREUZ: And what if he didn't do it?

DEFENSE COUNSEL: This question is of secondary importance to the principal significance of the death penalty. We want to abolish it because we don't want to run the risk of harming an innocent man, for that would trouble our serenity and our good conscience. In reality, however, the will to annihilate is as much our primal instinct as our will to live. Even if the death penalty has long been abolished, it will still lurk within us, ready to spring out at a given moment. It is the manifestation of primal instinct, and hence indestructible. But for centuries we have no greater care than to cage the beast in us, to prevent still further outbreaks. Here the monstrous significance of the State-sanctioned death penalty becomes manifest. There is a door in us, which we cannot slam in the face of our beast, because the representative power of morality, the State, holds it open with its own hand. Of course we can never slay the beast entirely. Remember that our ancestors lived in forests. [*Laughs.*] We are still living in forests. Think about that.

FISTELKREUZ: Sure, I've got nothing better to do.

DEFENSE COUNSEL: Bravo. As soon as our ancestors come to mind, we are right to busy ourselves with other things.

FISTELKREUZ: Still, a man shouldn't live like a beast.

DEFENSE COUNSEL: And have you safeguarded the gramophone?

FISTELKREUZ: Four months' rent is in arrears.

DEFENSE COUNSEL: The question remains open as to whether you are really entitled to treat him as a tenant.

FISTELKREUZ: I don't get it.

DEFENSE COUNSEL: Suppose the case got less clear-cut. That the trial lasted three times as long. Your claim for rent since his sentencing is more than dubious.

FISTELKREUZ [*threatening*]: Don't get nasty, sir.

DEFENSE COUNSEL [*sharply*]: I suggest that you turn the gramophone over to me in three days' time, or else I shall take the necessary steps against you.

FISTELKREUZ [*furious*]: We'll see about that.

DEFENSE COUNSEL [*furious*]: I'm acting in the interests of my client.

FISTELKREUZ: What's it to him when he's lying in the morgue?

DEFENSE COUNSEL: The court costs have to be paid.

FISTELKREUZ: People had better keep clear of you.

DEFENSE COUNSEL: Let's carry on. Table and chest of drawers, twenty marks.

FISTELKREUZ: I've got to have my rent.

DEFENSE COUNSEL: What's on top of the dresser?

FISTELKREUZ: Mirror, straight razor, brush.

DEFENSE COUNSEL: I'll put down two marks, fifty.

FISTELKREUZ: There's a crack in the washbasin.

[*Area 3 goes dark.*]

[*Simultaneously, area 5,* FRAU BERLESSEN'*s living room, lights up.*]

[*At a luxuriously laid table* JOSEF *and* TWO LADIES; JOSEF *is pouring wine in the* FIRST LADY'*s mouth.*]

FIRST LADY: I'm choking.

JOSEF [*laughs*]: You've got to do something for my money.

[SECOND LADY *laughs.*]

JOSEF: Go ahead and laugh. Soon you'll have something else in your
   mouth.

[*Laughter, eating, drinking.*]

[*Area 5 remains lit.*]

[*Simultaneously, area 1,* FRAU VON WIEG'*s room, lights up.*]

[OTTFRIED; *a* YOUNG MAN.]

OTTFRIED [*laughs*]: There's no need to feel inhibited. Barriers are
   made to be breached. More tea? [*Pours it out.*]

[*Area 1 goes dark.*]

[*Simultaneously, area 4,* ALFRED FISCHAU'*s room, lights up.* FRANK
is in ALFRED'*s room.*]

[*Two* POLICE INSPECTORS *enter.*]

FIRST POLICE INSPECTOR: We managed to get in without any fuss.

[FRANK *jumps up*.]

FIRST FIRST POLICE INSPECTOR: Herr Frank Berlessen?

FRANK [*quietly*]: Yes.

FIRST POLICE INSPECTOR: May we ask you to follow us.

[*Both* POLICE INSPECTORS *show their badges*.]

FRANK [*calmly*]: I've been expecting you. May I get my hat and coat?

FIRST POLICE INSPECTOR: Of course. We'll go with you.

[FRANK *and the two* POLICE INSPECTORS *exit*.]

[*The stage remains lit*.]

[*Jazz band, loud*.]

[*Area 7, the backroom of* KUDEKLA's *bar, lights up; music and dancing in full swing. At a table are* CARLA, BEN SIM, *and a* WOMAN.]

CARLA: What if something goes wrong?

WOMAN: Not with me. Two hundred marks.

CARLA: If I had two hundred marks, I'd keep the kid.

WOMAN: Then keep it.

BEN SIM: One way or another, she'll find the money. No need to get excited.

CARLA [*resolved*]: I'm getting fifty marks tomorrow.

BEN SIM [*laughs*]: Never give women an inch.

WOMAN: You can pay the rest in monthly installments.

BEN SIM: Waiter, two slivovitzes.

[*Area 7 remains lit.*]

[JOSEF, *in area 5, has meanwhile been called into the kitchen several times; now he leaves the* TWO LADIES.]

[*Lights up in area 1.*]

OTTFRIED: You can hear it even in here.

YOUNG MAN: Isn't that the bar that had the murder?

OTTFRIED: Who remembers that? Come on.

[OTTFRIED *and the* YOUNG MAN *dance together.*]

[*Area 6, the kitchen, lights up.*]

JOSEF: The cook is already in bed. She's locked herself in! [*Laughs.*] The other one's probably in bed with her boxer.

FIRST LADY [*laughs*]: We'll serve ourselves.

JOSEF [*laughs*]: Tomorrow they're both out of here.

[*Lights up again in area 3. Area 1 remains dark.*]

DEFENSE COUNSEL [*looking over the inventory, laughing*]: You don't get a legacy like this every day.

[JOSEF, OTTFRIED, *the* DEFENSE COUNSEL *and* BEN SIM *are now laughing simultaneously.*]

[*Area 2,* OLGA NAGERLE'*s room, lights up.* KUMMERER *reads from his manuscript.*]

KUMMERER: "As outsiders, we are making a mistake in our thinking. We grant a criminal trial a public, moral value. But the moral value is applicable to life, while sentencing and punishment arise from an entirely different context—from the context of the court of laws. That is a context unto itself. A world, which lies entirely elsewhere from life, a self-contained world, petrified for centuries. How is it possible that it has such power over us that it petrifies us the way an unexorcized ghost does small children, that its magical absurdity attracts us and we cannot escape it despite all our efforts?" [*Meditates.*]

[FRANK, *in hat and coat, reenters area 4 (*ALFRED FISCHAU*'s room) again with the* FIRST POLICE INSPECTOR *and the* SECOND POLICE INSPECTOR.]

FRANK: I'll just pick out a couple of books.

FIRST POLICE INSPECTOR: We can spare a couple of minutes.

FRANK: You're very kind.

KUMMERER [*goes on reading*]: "Because the judge in us expects it, a very severe judge, whom we should like to escape. What is the public prosecutor compared to the accuser within ourselves? So long as our Self cannot say no, the menacing *no* of the State remains ineffective and will never prevent those actions which we provisionally continue to call crimes. But we are too weak for the *no* of the Self, because we are human beings, in need of a compass and irresolute, and so we have created the punitive authorities so that they can soothe our conscience and lull our soul to sleep while we fear ourselves. Here, in this escape from ourselves, lies the indestructible power of institutional justice. We cannot run away from it, for its chains are in ourselves. But we could fight it step by step, and thus reconquer our soul." [*Looks up, very simply*] I will work, step by step, I will not despair. These eight years will soon be over—everything, everything will go on.

[*All the areas remain lit.*]

[*The music blares.*]

[*END.*]